Trut

A Manual for Whistle Blowers and Hell Raisers

The Theory and Practice of Letting Your Truth and
The Truth Prevail

Published by Kevin D. Annett, M.A., M.Div.
with the support of the International Tribunal of
Crimes of Church and State (ITCCS)

September 1, 2016

Table of Contents

Preface: Our Situation

No matter who you are or whatever your story, you have been drafted against your will into a controlled and regimented global corporate society over which you seem to have no control. Your allotted purpose in life is to serve that system unquestioningly with your labor, energy and taxes until the moment you are expendable. Deviate from that purpose and you will become a target.

As long as you remain within that little corral that you believe is your life, you can enjoy certain restricted "rights" - provided you don't challenge the way things are.

You may routinely hand over your authority to others with a mark on a ballot and call that "democracy". You may enjoy "freedom of speech and conscience" provided you don't act on what you believe. You can own your own home and bank account as long as someone richer than you holds the title to it all.

Those who live off your labor and set the rules that harness your life are selfish, invisible and unaccountable people; but even they are components of a soulless and murderous corporate machine that has no single ruler. That machine lives only to profit and sustain itself so that it can engulf and consume everything and everyone on our planet. It is a Thing that is out of control and reeking havoc and destruction on our species and all life.

Our situation, in other words, is desperate. Our very survival as humanity is at stake. In such a setting, either our daily priorities must change, or we must collectively die.

What matters now more than anything is the fight to reclaim our world by saying no to the corporate machine. But to do that, we must first reclaim our own minds and lives.

Enter the Truth Warrior.

Call them Whistle Blowers, Freedom Fighters or just plain Truthers: they are the men and women who have broken or are breaking free from the corral and tossing aside their mental shackles. They are the ones who live not according to the fear of what they might lose if they act, but the abhorrence of what we will all suffer if they do not.

This Manual is dedicated to such people, to the ones who made them so, and to those others to come who will be inspired and activated by them. If we will ever have a future of active liberty free of oppression and violence, it will be because of such resolute and courageous souls.

You know who you are. Take from this cup, drink, and carry on humanity's oldest battle. Or in the words of poet Percy Shelley, that Victorian-era Hell Raiser and lover of freedom,

"Rise like Lions after slumber, in unvanquishable number; Shake your chains to earth like dew, which in sleep had fallen on you. Ye are Many; They are Few"

Preamble: How to Use this Manual

If the sun comes up tomorrow it is only because of people of good will. And that's all that stands between us and the Devil. - Kenneth O'Donnell

The truth teller is entrusted with the soul of a people, without which they must die from the inside out. But this same truther is also the one most feared and shunned by the same people. This paradox is part of the hard and inescapable reality that has found you.

Having been under the gun from powerful institutions for over two decades has earned me some qualification to write this handbook. But my real education didn't happen overnight, and in order to survive I had to relearn everything I thought was true.

As a young United Church of Canada clergyman and "happy family man", I was blind to the corporate entity I was a part of until it reached out and destroyed my life. But even when it attacked me, I continually denied what was happening to me because it was too fantastic and horrible to believe. Denial is a primary defence mechanism of the human mind and of entire communities; and I indulged in it, unswervingly, even as my world was being destroyed.

My greatest problem back then was that I refused to learn from my own experience. Mentally disarmed by my own denial, I was bushwhacked time and again, and was nearly overwhelmed by those who wanted me dead and forgotten.

The face and the methods of war never change; only the circumstances and actors.

Every powerful institution on our planet is led and run by functional psychopaths who must subordinate every human feeling and restraint to the dual corporate goals of efficiency and self-preservation. There are no exceptions, from governments to private companies to churches and the military. Once you run afoul of such a system, and you show that you can't or won't cooperate with its inhuman requirements, then how that machine seeks either your compliance or your destruction will follow a predictable pattern and method.

In the darkness that is descending or will descend on you, your own experience, your inner stamina and your unsullied common sense are your best guides and weapons, now and in the times to come. In the new conditions that are your life, there is no-one for you to trust except yourself, and whatever greater power you believe in. Regardless of your faith, or lack of it, you must become your own Gospel and compass.

Foremost, you must learn hard realism. See everything and every person as they are, and not as you want them to be. To see and understand clearly is far more difficult than you can first realize, since we have all been raised in a culture of duplicity and false appearance. Children are taught to lie, evade and adapt, and to not speak what they know is true. For you, the first and most difficult step will be to look reality square in the face and not lie to yourself anymore.

No-one normally desires to look at painful truths, even when they are striking one down, and you are no exception. At every point in the disintegration of your old life you will struggle to cling to it and not want to accept the truth of what has befallen you.

You will tend to look to someone other than yourself to succor or even deliver you, for that is how you have been taught to think. That makes you even more vulnerable - especially at the hands of your new adversary.

In that sense, and above all, never look to your adversary to provide you with a way out of your sudden dilemma. You must never become deluded by the pleasant pseudo-morality of your opponent.

No institution, religious or otherwise, operates according to its own stated values. The latter are gloss and window dressing designed to attract and deceive, but in practice any fixed morality or values are an impediment to the smooth operation of a corporate machine. You have become a threat to that system, and so now, like any inconvenient principle, you must go.

Every institution has but one imperative and bottom line: its corporate efficiency and survival. Everyone and everything else is subordinate to that purpose, and is expendable. If you fail to understand this basic systems dynamic governing your adversary, you are doomed from the start.

Being a soulless machine, the thing you face lives according to the lies, appearances and measures required to preserve its own power, and nothing more. This makes someone like you quite incomprehensible to it, just as how it operates makes no sense to you, as a moral being. Ask for justice or decency from it, and you will face a dead wall of indifference, hollow rhetoric or meaningless gestures. But threaten its operations and income, and it will suddenly notice you, and it will be forced to respond to you.

Understand, above all else, that you are now engaged in a permanent and unrelenting war. You must suddenly learn to think and respond as someone engaged in perpetual combat.

The rules of war have their own justification and dynamic, wholly unlike and incompatible with the ways of "normal" peace time. Learning to be at war requires a momentous shift, but one helped by learning from the past, like the lessons contained in the appended Rules and Art of War.

Ultimately, despite the hell that is descending on you or that will strike you soon, never forget that it is you who have the upper hand, regardless of the size and apparent power of your adversary, simply because that opponent is afraid of you.

The corporate entity is much more vulnerable than is the lone truth teller, not only because it knows it is guilty but due to the fact that it is huge and unwieldy, and can only respond in set and predictable ways. That gives you, as a free agent, a fundamental advantage over it. Properly goaded by you, your seemingly invincible enemy can become its own worst enemy, and turn out over time to be your unanticipated ally in your pursuit of justice.

Most of what you will need to learn to survive and triumph over your particular slice of the darkness you will acquire yourself, through your own solid experience. The latter never lies. You will become a veteran in good time, becoming your own best teacher and a guide to others who will come after you. Such practical experience forms the core of this Manual but it is only a general guide. Learning to judge all things for yourself and act in your own power is part of the new training you will receive as one engaged in a permanent warfare.

As someone under constant fire, you will either collapse from the pressure or become a hardened perfectionist who strives to never make a mistake or a misjudgment. That is a fallacy, of course, since it's only by your mistakes that you will strengthen and overcome everything thrown at you. Don't fear your errors; learn and grow from them.

Above all else, stay confident that all things have their expiry date: especially evil and wrong doing, which require tremendous amounts of energy to sustain. The truth and goodness are always simple and easy, provided we adhere to them. You can come out of your war a stronger and more radiant soul, having been refined by learning a hidden and sacred lesson: that what matters most in your life is unseen and incorruptible, and thereby worth struggling and dying for. Such an awareness and resolve will be able to cause mountains to move, as you will discover after countless days and longer nights.

Introduction - The Choice, meaning Your Choice

You've just encountered a wrong in your workplace, in the community or among your colleagues that you cannot tolerate or cooperate with. Worse, you may have been asked by your employer or someone in authority to deliberately conceal a criminal or immoral act, or remain quiet about something that you know is unconscionable, or may harm others.

So, what do you do?

If you're like most people, you'll do what you're told to do, and will then justify what you've done with the usual lies and rationales that will help you sleep at night. But since you're reading this Manual, you're not likely one of that herd. Perhaps, then, my question is superfluous, because you know what you'll do to this challenge: You won't go along with what is wrong. Or perhaps you've already said your no.

So now, prepare for the shit storm.

Even before you face overt opposition or repression, your choice to uncover malfeasance or to not cooperate in a wrong will quickly cause you to feel fear, as well as fear's sorry cousin, doubt.

If you disclose your choice to colleagues or those you consider friends, their counsel will be for you to protect yourself and not risk anything, regardless of what or who is at stake. Those you have known and trusted, perhaps for years, may suddenly become your opponent, and possibly your worst enemy. If you persist in your choice and blow the whistle on wrongdoing, you must quickly learn to operate and think for yourself, and do so quite alone.

Regardless of your personality, you have been raised in a culture that does not value personal ethical choice. You have been indoctrinated from infancy to go along to get along, not to offend or cause division, and to conform your choices to majority opinion, peer or parental approval, or orders from on high.

Making a choice over and against the status quo that threatens its smooth operation is perceived and responded to by "official society" as something repugnant, illegal, and even insane. The moment you do so you will become not only criticized and despised, but an outcast and a walking target. And there is no more unnerving an experience.

For you to contemplate let alone make such a choice to openly dissent will be your first hard step, since like many people you have likely internalized a sense that to make a choice against the status quo is wrong. All that you have learned and been taught will become the biggest barrier to following through on your choice. The invisible censor and policeman in your own head will be your first and most formidable opponent, and he must be faced, understood, and made to stand down. But to achieve that you will have to learn to think and act in a new way, which is never easy or straight forward.

Establishing a new paradigm or view of the world is never something that occurs abstractly or overnight. It is a long and painful process born of conflict and loss. You will come to see not only your own situation but perhaps all of reality in a totally different way. In the words of one whistle blower,

"Everything I knew has become a lie, and everything I am experiencing has become a nightmare."

Such a shift is part of the process of maturing as a free and independent man or woman, stripped of the illusions and shackles that once made you complicit in a murderous global Corporatocracy. Such maturation is a continual process, and is only assured by your capacity to constantly assess and learn from your own experiences.

To paraphrase George Bernard Shaw, you must learn to constitute the real hope for mankind by conforming the world to yourself, rather than yourself to the world. Doing so, you will know that your own liberated mind contains within it the full power and substance of creation, is a complete and self-governing entity, and can therefore judge and order all things for itself.

All of this magnificent growth may or may not follow from your first choice to say no and thereby no longer conform yourself to wrongdoing. Whether such a step occurs depends on your possession of some very simple human qualities: courage, resolve, compassion, and especially stubbornness. Ultimately, it will be your own character that will decide your fate.

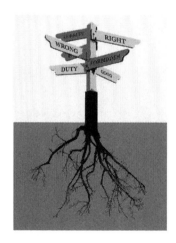

Chapter One: The Field of Battle

Only those who are under fire understand that a war is raging. - Karl von Clausewitz

First form the ground of conflict and thereby win victory before the battle has occurred. - Sun Tzu

Stage One: The Warning and the Offer

Homo Sapiens are the most adaptable species ever to live on planet Earth: a fact that is both a blessing and a curse. Our capacity to acclimatize and conform to every new environment and situation has allowed humanity to survive and thrive over hundreds of centuries. But that very flexibility has created a massive human tendency to habitually comply with whatever social and political order they find themselves in, and to allow any degree of brutality, injustice and tyranny to be perpetrated by their rulers on the many.

Why so many of us "go along to get along" with the status quo even when we know it is wrong can be speculated about from here to eternity. Whether such general acquiescence is due to an innate herd instinct, simple fear of punishment, or a conditioned indifference is not as important as the fact that this condition governs most of the people most of the time.

 Freedom does have its moments, and history does show that masses of people can occasionally and briefly wake up and throw off their shackles. But those rare and glorious moments do not govern what you and those like you will experience as truth warriors.

On the contrary.

As someone who cannot look the other way when wrong is occurring, you will quickly collide head on with an immovable, conservative mass of citizenry when you take your stand against a system of power. Yesterday's friends, colleagues and even family will overnight become today's adversaries, and your worst problem. Without warning or time to prepare, you will suddenly be thrown into a gladiatorial arena from which there seems to be no escape. And you will find that you have pathetically few weapons with which to conduct this unwanted and unforeseen battle.

Your first and biggest liability will be the fact that you are not only unshielded from what will attempt to crush you, but that you will not immediately realize the need for such a shield. For the first psychological response when one is assaulted is to deny that the attack is actually happening. *"This can't be happening to me! There must be some mistake!"* is the first thought of every whistle blower who has become a target.

You will typically be too shocked to respond to that first blow, or to even believe you are being accosted. Your disbelief in what is befalling you will disarm you. That is why the sudden, surprise attack is always the most effective one, and will invariably be used by your adversary against you.

Normally, any corporate adversary tries a softer initial approach to force a dissident back into line. Before the surprise attack on you will come the Warning and the Offer, an approach which is at its heart a sophisticated form of psychological warfare by your adversary designed to make you feel responsible for anything that may befall you.

The first stage of any corporate damage control in response to a whistle blower is normally to offer both an initial warning and an offer to the truther: the "steel fist clothed in a velvet glove" approach. This Warning-Offer is presented as a one time only "gift" to you, the so-called wayward employee, to psychologically pressure you to recant your position and return to the sheep fold, as in *"We're willing to overlook this little mishap and even give you certain benefits* (read: bribe) *but only if you stop what you're doing immediately."*

Normally, you will be given no more than forty eight hours to accept or refuse the adversary's one time offer. In law school, budding attorneys are taught that to control the outcome of a negotiation one must instill fear and defensiveness in one's opponent. Imposing arbitrary deadlines is a primary way of doing that. Time pressure will be brought to bear upon you after the offer is made, for under stress, logic and perspective give way to panic and impulse, which is what your adversary wants to instill in you to get you to go along with their deal.

Stay calm, in other words. Remember that you are holding the cards in this situation, for you are the one being bullied and coerced. If you weren't a threat you wouldn't be treated this way. You can control the outcome.

Practical Note No. 1: Record everything that happens in your encounters with the adversary, either with a recording device or by always having at least one eyewitness with you. This independent record is crucial for later battles and any possible legal fight you wage with them. Never meet alone with the adversary, for they will try overwhelming you in a gang or with lawyers present. If they refuse you the right to record what's happening, do so anyway.

As anyone does when suddenly under fire, you must learn how to bluff and maneuver, or be destroyed. Learn to camouflage your true intentions behind a mask of deception when dealing with your enemy. The Warning and Offer phase is the place to begin this *modus operandi.*

As tempting as it is, never respond from pride, indignation or anger to the cruelty and ultimatums of your adversary. They want you to react in this way and thereby lose hold of your own judgment. Keep a poker face with them at all times whether you are negotiating with them or not. Always appear and remain inwardly calm and dignified; never plead or appeal in desperation to them, for then they have won the psychological battle.

It is vital that you not be open and up front with your adversary or you will be outflanked and destroyed, since they will immediately know your intentions. First ask for more time to consider their offer. When they refuse, as they usually will, retire into the shadows and do not let them know what you are feeling or thinking.

The brief time allotted you to accept or reject their offer is the real moment of truth for you, not so much because of what the adversary is doing but because of the opening now afforded you to come to know yourself, and what it is you will and won't do. In "peaceful" times, we can never really come to know ourselves since all of our choices tend to be self-serving. But peace has passed away now, and you are in a crisis and at a turning point in your life. Thing are suddenly sharp and crystal clear.

Remember that every crisis is an opportunity: and in this case, the crisis presents a chance for you to lay aside your normal, conditioned tendency to consider all choices according to a relative measure of personal gain versus loss. Such a measure does not apply anymore, because no matter what choice you make, you will seem to lose, by "normal" standards. Set aside your ego and fear of loss, and ask yourself instead, what is the right thing to do? For now that is your only measure of things.

If you place rightness before all else, then your answer to the Offer will be no. And then the Assault will begin.

Stage Two: The Assault

Nothing will prepare you for the Assault. Nothing you have experienced until then will equip you to deal with it. At first it will roll over you like a Tsunami, and it may take weeks, even months, for you to land on your own feet again. But you will, and you will gain an inestimable gift in the process: the knowledge that you have a strength within you that you didn't know you possessed.

The Assault will begin the very moment that you refuse your adversary's offer.

The legal definition of Assault is *"any act or inference or implied threat that places one in a state of fear or concern for one's safety or well being"* (Black's Law Dictionary). The deadly looks given to you by the adversary; the threats they will make at you and your family if you reject their offer; even their silence and refusal to answer your questions are all forms of assault under the law. And having refused the adversary, you are now set squarely in their cross hairs and are considered by them to be a "legitimate target" for any amount of assault.

Your enemy operates according to a set institutional protocol, and at this point - the moment you present a direct challenge to them - their assault on you will be so immediate and relentless that you will feel overwhelmed and powerless. You will then be tempted to back down and accede to their demands on you.

We find that a majority of initial truth tellers cave in to this first stage of the assault because of its raw power and unexpected brutality. Your adversary relies on this fact to steer most dissidents back into line without the cost and hassle of the litigation or drawn out smear campaign that must follow if you hold out against them.

A standard scenario in their first big assault on you, after you have turned down their offer, will be to present you with a legal Letter of Demand or a Cease and Desist Notice. Normally these letters will be ready to hand to you the moment you say no to their offer. The adversary will threaten you with a huge lawsuit if you don't back down and agree to their demands, and again will give you a brief span of time in which to comply before threatening to commence litigation against you.

Letters from lawyers always tend to scare people. They are designed to do so, relying on peoples' ignorance of the law and due process to coerce them into line. But it is a standard maxim in the legal world that the threat of a lawsuit means that there will never be one. For those with power have no need to issue threats; they will simply act.

The truth is that a big institution has far more to lose in a legal fight than does a lone individual like you, since it puts at risk their two most precious things: their public reputation and money. So the best thing to do when handed such threatening letters is to cheerfully say to your opponent *"Bring it on!"*

Trust me, they won't. For even in their best case scenario, the adversary – by suing you and legally preventing you from speaking or acting - will simply bring immediate public attention to you and your cause, which is the one thing they don't want to do.

The truth is that the world loves a David and Goliath battle, and while the crowd is always fickle and their interest is momentary, in the brief exposure shone on you by such a lawsuit you will gain priceless attention from the media and well wishers who would never have known about you otherwise. This exposure is poisonous to your adversary, and they know it. That is why long before you ever go to trial they will try to buy you off with an out of court settlement consisting of some piddling amount of money and an accompanying "gag order" to permanently shut you up.

In reality, the adversary's lawyers and Public Relations drones will never let that happen in the first stages of their assault on you.

For a powerful opponent, a cheaper and more proven method of containing and then crushing truth tellers is to first attack those around them and destroy their local and then public reputation. So regardless of how you respond to their threats of litigation, the adversary will immediately start smearing and lying about you to everyone you know, starting with the people closest to you.

There is only one way to counter these smears, and that is for you to strike first with your own version of what has happened. *Tell your own story, define the issues at stake and thereby establish the terms of the battle before it ever begins.*

Sun Tzu calls this action "forming the ground" of a battle in order to set the conditions of the engagement and thereby ensure victory. To do so does not require great strength, simply cunning and initiative.

Public relations experts term this "defining the narrative" of an issue in order to present your own version of a certain reality to the world. If you do not do so, you will spend years digging yourself out from under the lies and misrepresentation foisted on you by your adversary, distracting your energy from your main purpose of exposing that same adversary.

Practical Note No. 2: Immediately issue to your community your own account of what has happened to you, naming the issues and the names of the wrongdoers. Seize and hold the moral high ground and define the story, before the adversary defines it for you to your ruin. Publish all your evidence and cold, hard facts, and keep the world informed about how your campaign unfolds.

Of course, defining the struggle on your terms will not by itself lessen the adversary's assault on you. But you must always return to the issue that prompted your exposure and avoid the fog of personal attacks, innuendo and gossip the adversary will continually create to distract from that issue.

In short, always stick to the issue.

Whenever you publicly and loudly attack what your opponent holds dear and take the offensive against their crimes and corruption, they <u>must</u> respond, no matter how small you are. In that way you can keep a much bigger opponent on the defensive and win yourself breathing space and the room to maneuver. This is one practical way to respond to the Assault.

Ultimately, there will be no substitute for your personal capacity to bear suffering and endure. And there will suddenly be more to endure than you can ever have imagined.

In the weeks and months after the first assault, you will begin to encounter the hatred and fear stare from people you've never met. Your name will be publicly dragged through the mud. Your funds will evaporate and you will become unemployable. You may be followed around by strangers. Your phone, mail and internet will be continually disrupted and sabotaged. You will receive death threats. You may lose your family and access to your children, since a common tactic used by damage-controlling corporations is to approach a whistle blower's spouse and offer them money to leave or divorce him. Most of all, you will come to realize that you are being constantly hunted, that you are always vulnerable, and that fewer and fewer people will give you any kind of support. This is a personally terrifying place to be.

Unlike a normal battle, these attacks will not cease. They will continue day after day without let up. The psychological strain on you will increase exponentially the longer you remain engaged with your adversary. And there will generally be no safe place to where you can withdraw.

Normally, if your adversary cannot crush you within a brief span of time – say, if you hold out and persist over six months after your initial victimization – their strategy will shift from one of overt assault to that of socially isolating you through prolonged psychological warfare. They will strive to ensure that no-one will ever listen to you or associate with you by casting such a negative hue around you that your message and evidence will be ignored.

All of this is something I call **The Siege**. It is by far the most potent weapon in your adversary's arsenal.

Stage Three: Enduring the Seige

Surviving a siege requires a defensive stance but not defensive thinking, for the attacking enemy must be disrupted and drawn into fatal engagements wherever possible. Nevertheless, three qualities by the defenders are required to outlast any siege: secure and bountiful supplies, solid ramparts and an outside relieving force to to raise the siege. The absence of any of these three factors will eventually cause the defenders to be overcome. - Sun Tzu, The Art of War

If their initial assault on you has not forced your collapse, and in precisely the same manner and attitude of a besieging army, your adversary will surround and isolate you in order to batter you into submission. They will attempt to wear you down by drying up all of your support, wearing down your defenses, and making any relief impossible. They will assume that their own position as the attacker is supreme and unchallengeable. But this hubris on their part is also a great weakness and can be exploited by you, even while you are being besieged.

Your adversary's strategy at this point is simple: to render you materially and psychologically isolated from the rest of society and scare away from you any support. Their methods are designed to sow widespread doubt and disbelief about you and your cause, and de-legitimate both. At first they will do so very effectively because of the fear and suspicion that can be ignited in a population that is already pre-disposed to think the worst of a public or "controversial" figure like you, especially if you are a Caucasian male.

Thanks to their big bank account, your adversary will destroy your ability to earn a living and make you unemployable.

This will happen through the power of rumor and character assassination, aided by the all-penetrating medium of the internet. The adversary will set up or hire a special "Black Ops" team that issues false (or "blind") stories and misinformation about you to the media, to academics, politicians, lawyers, social activists and any group of people to whom you are especially appealing or who might pick up your cause.

To these potential supporters of yours the Black Ops team will publicly accuse you of at least one if not all three of these offenses: mental and emotional instability and a chronic tendency to lie, financial improprieties, or sexual deviancy. These lies are designed to cause confusion and doubt about you that will cause even your closest supporters to drop away from you with the attitude that you're "not worth the hassle".

Chapter Three ("*Knowing your Adversary*") goes into more detail about the nature of such character assassination programs and how finely tuned they are in the hands of the state and other large corporations. Suffice it to say that these campaigns to murder your good name always work, at least in the short run. They can be endured and overcome eventually if you have a very tough skin, a deep belief in yourself and a will of iron, but initially these smears will normally destroy any support network that has built up around you. This is simply because your supporters will have no experience of what is assaulting their psyches. They will not be able to accept the fact that they are being targeted by a colossal lying machine that knows where to aim at the human psyche to generate maximum fear, confusion and division.

The devastating power of The Siege lies in how entrenched and unshakeable it becomes over time. Not all of this is the result of overt acts or the regime of general isolation set up by your adversary. Some of it arises from the extremity of your new situation and the wear and tear on your heart and mind caused by living so alone, vilified and ignored for so long. In some ways, there is no more terrible fate for a man or woman than to be publicly shunned, for we are at bottom social creatures who need one another.

Over time, even the strongest truth teller with the most resolute commitment can begin to internalize the lies and ostracism inflicted on him. A hidden voice within you begins to utter, *"If so many people hate and fear me, maybe I have done something wrong"*. And the longer you endure social ostracism the more your self-doubts will grow. All of this is part of your adversary's game plan, for they know that to prompt your own self-destruction is more beneficial to them than to make you a martyr by openly destroying you.

To break a siege one must push out from a surrounded position or be rescued from without, or both. That's the theory. In practice, an isolated truth teller who is hemmed in by lies, attacks and smears is reduced to defending himself all the time, which tends to prompt inward looking, self-justifying behavior that only serves the adversary.

Those who have suffered for exposing a wrong tend to become extreme individualists who are incapable of trusting or working with others, often for good reasons. The wider world cannot understand this particular ordeal of the truth telling prophet, who to them appears simply to be eccentric, aloof or paranoid.

In many ways, this distance between you and the world makes it difficult for even allies of yours to approach or stand with you, as a lone warrior. All of this is what your adversary uses to keep you and the dangerous truth marginalized and forgotten.

Frankly, while it is possible to survive such a siege with your mind and the truth intact – even if hardly anyone knows about it - it is against the odds to break such an encirclement and throw back one's adversary, and defeat your opponent. The good guys only win in Hollywood. In reality, the best case scenario we can usually come up with is a stalemate, for we are up against powerful corporate bodies that are in practice above the law and unaccountable.

The truth is that on a personal level, whistle blowers can never really recover from their ordeal. We are never fully vindicated or believed, even when what we have exposed is validated and proven right. A shadow and stigma will always hang over us, and we will bear for all our days the mark of the brutality we have endured. Being under fire always permanently changes a human being.

That said, the best way to reduce the siege you find yourself in is to always strive to keep your adversary on the defensive. Do not stand on your initial action alone; never stop digging, turning up new damning evidence, and broadcasting it to the world. In whatever ways you can, keep shoving the raw truth and its evidence in the face of the adversary and the world. Do so calmly, with hard facts and not hearsay or opinion, and with the voice of a seasoned and sage veteran. Do so consistently and you will not only prove your credibility but the adversary must divert some of his attack from you to defending themselves.

Practical Note No. 3: When your back is against the wall, attack: not once or twice, but constantly. Do so vocally and publicly. The smaller you are the louder must be your voice. Protest on the terrain of whatever your adversary holds to be most sacred. Directly threaten what they love and their pressure on you will slacken. Be audacious and always do the unexpected thing. Cause a shock but do so armed with irrefutable facts and damning evidence. Even your strongest opponent will then be forced on to the defensive.

When outnumbered and surrounded by three Panzer divisions at Bastogne during the Battle of the Bulge in 1944, US Army General Anthony MacAuliffe commented laconically to his officers, *"So they've got us surrounded, the poor bastards!"*

This was not simply plucky defiance, but sound military logic. For by diverting so much firepower to reduce Bastogne, the Nazi commanders lost sight of their bigger objective and so delayed their timetable that other Allied armies were able to block and finally overwhelm them. MacAuliffe could see the bigger picture the enemy could not.

You must be likewise. Never let the fierceness or power of the adversary's assault or besieging of you make you lose sight of the fact that the longer you hold your position the more you weaken the enemy. Time is always on the side of truth.

In general, let the adversary expend himself by attacking you. Keep the moral and truthful high ground and no encirclement can destroy you, for the universe bends towards what is true: and humanity will see that by your very endurance and courage you are legitimate and are speaking the truth. That in itself may be your greatest victory.

If you know the enemy
and know yourself
you need not fear the
results of a hundred battles.

-- Sun Tzu --

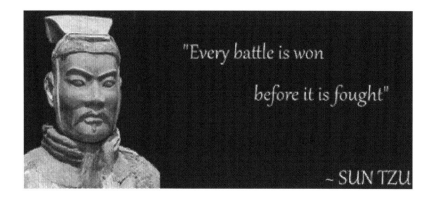

"Every battle is won before it is fought"

~ SUN TZU

Chapter Two: Your Response

"So what do I do now?"

This is the big question facing you after the big boot has crashed down on your life. How are you to respond to not just the attacks of a ruthless adversary, but the crushing need to bring your truth to the world? Can you actually win justice and vindication in the midst of such a firestorm?

No-one who has become targeted for destruction ever believes at first that it is really happening to them, or that it will endure for very long. One is convinced that some terrible mistake has been made and that rightness will correct everything soon.

Despite how clearly experience quickly proves the opposite, our habitual view of the world – that things are basically just and orderly - prevents us from acknowledging our own experience: namely, that we are being methodically and deliberately destroyed by flesh and blood others who have become their own law.

Our first and biggest enemy is not those others, but ourselves: specifically, our own naivete and illusions about what is happening to us and what can be done about it.

Shedding false ideas is terribly slow and painful at the best of times, but under the assaults you are facing or will face, doing so is an imperative, a matter of life and death. For nothing can be done by you against the evil you face as long as you wear a blindfold.

Depositing Your Illusions and Learning Total Realism

*Self-delusion is the most tenacious quality in the human mind.
History teaches but it has no pupils.* - Antonio Gramsci, 1931

One of the most difficult parts of learning to live as an assaulted truth teller is that one must reassess one's entire world view, for nothing makes sense any more. Long before you become an exile from the world you knew, your sense of that reality will start to crumble.

Once you go up against a big corporate institution, none of the former solutions will work, for there will be no help for you from the police, the media, or anyone you once relied on. You will discover up close and quickly how tenuous are your relationships, and how a whiff of danger or controversy will blow away your friends and even family members. You will painfully discover how with most people fear is normally stronger than love, integrity or courage.

That is indeed an agonizing discovery, and it will be one you reject at first with the kind of denial that is a natural psychological defense against death and dying. For in truth you are experiencing the death of an old life and its assumptions.

The process of dying has distinct stages that embrace disorientation, denial, outrage, desperation, letting go and a final acceptance. Many people are not able to pass through all of these stages before their physical ending because they deny their own reality. Truth tellers too can find it impossible to adjust to their new reality and die to their old life in order to embrace a new one.

We find that those who can make this transition are people who are capable of a humble self-realization and who possess the inner strength to accept their own nature. When Mohandas Gandhi observed, *"The seeker of truth must be as humble as dust"*, he could have been referring to prophets and whistle blowers. But we can add to Gandhi's aphorism that such seekers must also be total realists and forgo all fanciful and self-serving thinking. For we must first face the truth of who we are and not who we imagine ourselves to be if we are to endure the collapse of our old life and avoid a sterile personal regret and bitterness that can blind us even more.

Being honest is a crucial aspect of knowing how to respond to the attacks you are facing, because your tendency will be to operate with a habitual mentality to such attacks, and look for a quick and easy solution. You will be tempted (and will undoubtedly be advised) to seek legal assistance or enter into negotiations with your adversary. You will want to play by the rules you have known up until then and that have always worked for you. But if you do so you will fail, for you have not yet learned the reality of your new situation.

<u>Practical Note No. 4:</u> At this stage of your battle, start keeping a personal journal, if you don't do so already, in which you record the intimate details of what you are dreaming, imagining, hoping and fearing. This is vital, not just as an historical record but by examining your own thoughts and helping to rid yourself of fallacies and attitudes that stand in your way. You can face your inner questions, like "Can this really be happening to me? Why am I incapable of accepting the truth?" And so on.

Going for their Jugular

In the first phase of their assault on in-house dissidents like you, your opponent's protocol is to play on your fears and illusions by appearing to want to play ball with you and negotiate your differences. *They are doing so to stall you and win the time they need to cover up the dirt you have uncovered, as well as to silence your potential witnesses or supporters.*

Your enemy needs this initial period of time to bury the evidence. You will accordingly be strung along for weeks or months and given various false rays of hope to keep you from doing what your adversary fears, which is to go public and expose them early on, when they haven't fully covered up their wrong doing.

The truth is that a big corporate entity is most vulnerable immediately after an exposure of their wrong doing. The longer one waits to attack them publicly, the less likely will be any chance of exposure, since the money is on their side and will quickly shut off your options. What such a colossal enemy doesn't expect is for you to splash the truth that you've discovered all over the place right away. They expect you to be cautious, self-preoccupied and wary, especially after they start threatening and attacking you.

This is where you need to know Sun Tzu's *The Art of War* by heart and become an instinctive guerrilla warrior. For you must respond to your adversary with the immediate cunning, unpredictability and swiftness that Sun Tzu prescribes to any small force encountering a larger opponent. (*See Appendix Two*)

Put simply, you must go for your adversary's jugular as quickly and as unexpectedly as possible. You must make up what you lack in size with audacity and force.

How does one person or a handful of people "go for the jugular" of a big company or government? Quite simply, you embarrass the crap out of your adversary, whose double-edged Achilles' Heel is always their public image and their money.

To give some real life examples of this method that have worked against big corporations:

- Child-killing churches are confronted by silent protestors standing up in the Sunday service with the names of the murdered children, and parishioners are leafleted and urged not to donate to the church.

- Toxic-dumping corporations have waste strewn about the front lobby of their corporate headquarters and are presented with a bill for damages to your community.

- The names and faces of child raping priests are posted all about their church and community, and it is announced that citizen arrests will be performed on the perpetrators.

In all of these cases, once the media reported these protest actions, the bigger adversary collapsed publicly within a matter of a week. The bottom line to gaining such tactical victories was that these groups published the facts and the evidence of the crimes that they uncovered in a way that cost their opponent maximum revenue and embarrassment. You must always seek to do the same, as soon as possible.

Your best weapon in publicly shaming your opponent is not only the truth itself, which you must publicly announce over and over; it is also creating the biggest conflict possible to scare your adversary into thinking of how much they will lose in a drawn out battle with you. But of course this is all dependent on you getting the story out publicly, whether through the "mainstream" media or your own.

Let's say, on the other hand, that you're not the "protesting" type. Maybe you hate conflict and want things to work out reasonably. If so, then I'm afraid you're in for a lot of grief and disappointment. As a persecuted truth teller you will never be given anything by your opponent except pain: they are out to either make you comply or destroy you. The only question is, how do you plan to defend yourself and what you love?

Because you are under fire, what will not be obvious to you right away is the fact that you actually have much more power in this situation than you realize. You can damage your adversary far more than they can damage you. Your fears and pre-conditioned subservience will be trying to convince you otherwise. But there is nothing more de-stabilizing to a big corporate body than their dirty laundry being aired by someone like you who now has nothing left to lose.

As Sun Tzu observes,

"Hopeless situations are your best ally. Hostile ground heightens your focus. Place yourself where you cannot leave. Facing death, you will find your true strength and profound inner power. No training can prepare you for this. Dire circumstances evoke it, unsought yet attained. The right emergency unleashes enormous power in you greater than your individual parts."

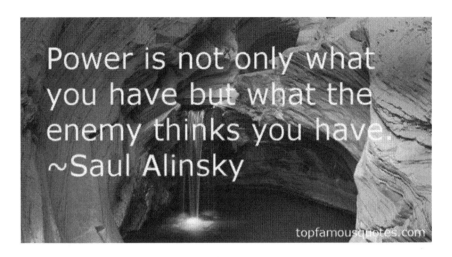

Power is not only what you have but what the enemy thinks you have.
~Saul Alinsky

topfamousquotes.com

Organizing your Supporters and Building a Broader Movement

Every whistle blower longs to see their adversary exposed and beaten, and justice triumph. It's a nice idea. But the immediate, practical question is always how does one gather the force to compel such an outcome?

You have begun your struggle alone through an act of conscience, and in many ways you will remain alone in your own truth and travail. In your present situation, Fate has chosen you to make a choice and do what no-one else can or will do. That makes you the spear head and symbol of your campaign, and you must never relinquish that role. But you also need people around you, for your protection, sustenance and ultimate victory. You need wherever possible to build a broader movement to oppose the evils you have revealed and fight to abolish them. Your adversary fears such numbers.

Of course, building and maintaining any kind of social-political movement, especially in the face of a powerful adversary, is much easier said than done.

The first problem is that nobody else understands the issue like you do, and even your supporters who haven't been scared off by the odds you face need to be brought up to speed about all the facts, events and issues involved. You will find that you must be constantly briefing and educating your own people. Doing so is a constantly exhausting process and will be extremely difficult to sustain when you are also fighting off the latest blows from your adversary and trying to survive against enormous odds.

That is, as you generate a broader movement around your issue you will face the "Chief Cook and Bottle Washer" dilemma where you are forced to be the leader, administrator, educator, public speaker and main organizer of your new movement. Trying to keep all those balls in the air at once quickly dissipates your energy and prevents you from doing any of them effectively.

Social movements also reflect the limitations of their weakest elements, and are constantly impeded by the Lowest Common Denominator Factor of democracy: that your group can move only as fast and as far as the least aware and engaged person in your ranks. **Such a restriction is fatal under the harsh conditions of war.** For as Sun Tzu reminds us,

Whoever depends on a majority for victory must reflect its weakest aspects and must thereby be defeated. Seasoned minorities alone are capable of sustained and purposeful action and thereby, victory. Only veterans are capable of victorious combat, by leading the inexperienced or wavering mass in their wake. The leadership of this vanguard of veterans is the key to victory in every battle.

Flowing from this, it becomes clear that the best method for cutting-edge truth tellers like yourself is not to build a large, unwieldy organization but rather small, educated and disciplined action groups that can assault your enemy without the liability of the weakest elements.

Large groups are easily monitored, infiltrated and destroyed from within, as many of us have experienced time and again. But guerrilla squads of three to five people can harass your adversary with unexpected protests and then fade into the shadows, presenting no visible target to retaliate against. This tends to strike fear and uncertainty among your enemies.

At the same time, small groups don't mean your aims or impact have to remain small. On the contrary, your voice must sound like you represent a million and more people, which of course you do: all of those who suffer or will suffer from the deeds of your adversary. Your movement must be loud and disruptive, but organizationally tight, closed and action-oriented.

That is, as community organizer Saul Alinsky observed as the First Rule for Activists, *"Power is not only what you have but what your enemy thinks you have"*. *That maxim must always be borne in mind and direct all that you do.*

Between 2005 and 2008, Canada finally buckled and began acknowledging the Indian residential school crimes because barely two dozen members of our network had so dominated the issue by our protests and occupations inside and outside the guilty churches that we forced media attention and a response from our adversaries.

These events proved once again the old adage that numbers is never the ultimate issue in warfare, but rather audacity, will, and strategic action at the right moment and place. Then your impact will far exceed your physical power.

In the long run, what matters is not only your personal witness on an issue but how that stand can translate itself into a more general campaign against the forces responsible for the crimes you have exposed. How you forge that campaign into a spear to drive into the heart of your adversary cannot be pre-ordained, but must be determined as your movement develops.

At the same time, standing in total realism, you must also expect the crowd – and even loyal supporters - to desert you when the boot comes down and the glamour of your stand fades. Above all else, you must learn to stand alone and carry on when everyone is against you. *"For the clarity and the will of the commander is the critical factor in deciding any battle".* (Sun Tzu)

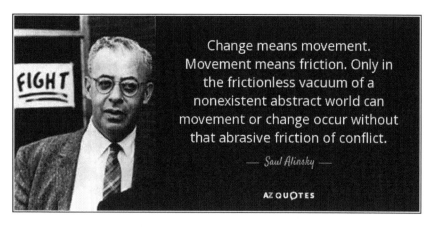

Change means movement. Movement means friction. Only in the frictionless vacuum of a nonexistent abstract world can movement or change occur without that abrasive friction of conflict.

— *Saul Alinsky* —

AZ QUOTES

Learning the Sniper's Trade: The Advantage of Being Small, Mobile and Unpredictable

Let your plans be as dark as night, then strike like a thunderbolt with utter surprise. For when you are few and the enemy is many, you can use the few to strike the many because those whom you battle are restricted, being larger and more unwieldy. A single shot from out of the dark is more frightening to such an opponent than a hundred shots in daylight. - Sun Tzu, *The Art of War*

Before you became a hunted person, you could call a meeting and a hundred people might show up. People listened to you without fear. Now, you'll be lucky to draw the attention or support of three or four people. You are essentially alone. You have no army except the invisible kind. You are not leading a major counter-assault by a big army but instead are taking shots at your adversary wherever you can.

Such is the tactical position of the whistle blower. You are in effect a sniper.

It's important to keep in mind such a humbly realistic sense of scale and of self when you start striking back at your opponent. You do not command an army. And since you are suddenly in the sniper's trade, what matters most is the accuracy and the strategic timing and placing of your shots.

One of your advantages in your situation is that you are facing an enormous target that can't budge. Unlike you, your corporate adversary cannot maneuver or be supple in their methods. Their movements are fixed and predictable, and they are governed by the fear of loss. Therein lies a big part of their vulnerability.

A single well placed shot by you can have a tremendous impact on such an opponent far beyond the caliber of your weapon. A case in point: At the first public protest I held soon after my firing without cause by the United Church of Canada in 1995, an aboriginal participant at the rally was quoted in the *Vancouver Sun* newspaper as having seen the killing of a child at that church's Alberni residential school. The next morning, the national office of the United Church issued a hurried press statement claiming ignorance of the child's death and denying that they had covered up the incident. But at that point, no-one had even accused them of a cover up!

This incident is a classic example of the power truth tellers hold because of the latent guilt and paranoia of a big criminal institution: a body that can be easily prodded to over react and expose itself by a single shot from our direction.

The venerable community organizer Saul Alinsky, in his seminal book Rules for Radicals (1971), states as one of his maxims that "Your enemy, properly goaded, can be your best ally. The bigger they are, the more quickly and stupidly they tend to react to a threat." By provoking your opponent you learn to discern his aims and weakness, and force him to reveal himself. To quote Sun Tzu, "Prick them to know their movement. Probe them to know their strength and deficiency."

Practical Note No. 5: In your public statements and protests, give your issue a human face, and always get personal about your enemy. Name the CEO responsible for your victimization, expose his wrongdoing and challenge him to come out from behind his lawyers and flunkies and face you. Wherever you can, laugh at and deride your big opponent and his deeds, since no-one in 'authority' can bear being publicly ridiculed. All of this will provoke your adversary to make rash mistakes, appear stupid and blurt out things they shouldn't, which only serves to de-legitimate them in the public eye. Always prod and provoke, and forget about being nice about it!

Such irreverent methods can rebound in your favor since they gain you a reputation for irreverence, humor and courage that attracts others to you and your cause. For ultimately you can only lead by example and your own demonstrated integrity when all your other means have been stripped away.

Yet another example of this was discovered in the late 1990's in Vancouver as aboriginal people began responding to my continual campaigning on the issue of missing and murdered residential school children. Eventually fifty or more natives would start appearing at my formerly-miniscule protests outside the downtown churches that ran the 'schools'.

But our power lay partly in the fact that we never announced what church we would strike next, or what we would be doing there; sometimes we merely picketed, other times we went into the church service and leafleted the congregation, or made impromptu speeches from the pulpit.

This unpredictability and daring created a wonderful paranoia and fear among the staff and head officers of those churches and created hilarious theater. These spectacles achieved what every corporate PR specialist dreads: public notoriety.

By our actions, a limelight was fastened on the guilty churches and the fact of their murder of countless children. Eventually even the corporate media was forced to report our actions and the crimes of the churches, especially as we gave a voice to the eyewitnesses who showed up at our regular church actions.

The success of a few of us in eventually forcing the truth of genocide by Canadian church and state into the light of day was the result of the inability of those institutions to contain or overcome our guerrilla methods. Accordingly, these bodies were forced to respond on our terms to the issue they wanted to avoid, for over years we had worn down their morale and energy by our unpredictable striking at the thing they valued the most: their Sunday worship services and the cash they generate.

This form of mobile guerrilla warfare is precisely the method a truth teller and his meager forces must rely on to start turning the tables on the powerful.

In Sun Tzu's words,

"Being fluid like a river and without permanent form, you compel your enemy to defend against you at every point. He is thereby dissipated and weakened, and kept ignorant of your purpose while forced to reveal his condition to you. Such weakness then breeds demoralization and collapse."

The War of Maneuver

Flowing from this guerrilla army stance is the recognition that most of our active engagement of our adversary does not consist of direct confrontation but of a constant ***war of maneuver*** in order to find the key moment and place at which to strike: the S*chwerpunkt* or "decisive point" in any battle.

The War of Maneuver is best understood by recognizing that in the natural order, power is not found in solid phenomena but in a constant energetic flow of relationships, which are always in a constant flux. The power of a squirrel to cross a river on a log lies neither in the log or the squirrel in themselves, but in their *temporary combination.* That brief union is their power.

Every human interaction and social conflict is the same way, and their outcome is determined not by fixed methods but by what momentary maneuver most effectively allows a sudden change in the power balance. A practical example of this lies in the tactic of the sit-in.

Devised spontaneously by American autoworkers during the big union organizing drives of the 1930's, the seizure of factories by the workers caught the plant owners off guard, terrifying and immobilizing them; not only because of the new and unexpected nature of the action but by its strategic seizure of property vital to the owners.

By these unexpected actions, the power relationship was suddenly reversed. And so within barely a few weeks of these occupations, the big auto manufacturers caved in to this tactic and signed the first industrial union contracts with their workers.

By the 1960's, when the sit-in was used almost habitually by student, anti-war and civil rights protestors, the system had learned to adapt to the action and create responses that deflated its power. University administrators were encouraged by the United States government to create "sit in areas" or rooms where protestors could safely "occupy" a marginal part of the campus that harmed and threatened nothing. Today there are actual "free speech zones" in many cities where protests are "allowed" and safely channeled.

This kind of ritualized action – like the standard Saturday stroll through a quiet downtown that some call a protest march – merely siphons off peoples' energy into dead end gestures, and leaves the status-quo power balance intact.

In short, yesterday's power-shifting method invariably becomes today's power-stabilizing action – but only because the participants are not recognizing that their war is primarily one of maneuver, constant change and flexibility until the right moment to strike emerges.

In the words once again of Saul Alinsky,

"Political struggle by the Have Nots must be ninety percent inspiration and ten percent routine, since those without institutional means have only their own creative ingenuity to rely on"

How does one begin a war of maneuver with a powerful adversary? Such movement, in truth, begins from the first moment of conflict. Your opponent will continually try to dominate you, control your thoughts and actions, and create a false narrative and chain of events surrounding what has happened to you.

In this vein, they will maneuver constantly to isolate and discredit you once you won't play ball with them, all the time expecting that you will simply react to their movements rather than launch your own.

Beginning your own maneuvering is in fact key to your survival and vindication. Do not wait for your adversary to strike; as described, seek to put them on the defensive and make them respond to the issues that you are defining as the real ones. To do so requires constant vigilance, focus and devotion by you. For unlike your life until then, your every waking moment must now be geared towards a single aim: battling the wrong done to you and the deeper evil that has caused it.

Such a totally consecrated life has its own strengths and set of problems, especially when it comes to your capacity to be watchful and maneuverable. For frankly, becoming wrapped up in one's own painful struggle and the crimes of a big adversary tends to make one self-absorbed, hard minded and rigidly inflexible, and bogged down in one set of actions. All of this works against your capacity to learn how to maneuver and learn from your own mistakes.

Habitual thinking is the greatest barrier to becoming a master of maneuver.

A classic example of this is the tendency for a just-dismissed employee to appeal the decision or file a grievance within the very company that expelled him. Even when every appeal fails and one level of the bureaucracy supports the next, the expelled employee will still keep battering away with protests to obscure officials. The very determination and will of such a person quickly becomes his worst enemy, for it traps him in a maze out of which he cannot maneuver.

It is a military maxim that a smaller force must yield space to an overwhelming attacker rather than engage with that power, in order to win the time and space to maneuver and allow the attacker to dissipate itself. This simple common sense truth must be discovered the hard way over and again by the recently victimized whistle blower, whose every impulse at first is to stubbornly resist and push back against what is trying to overwhelm him.

When Jesus said to *"not resist"* one's enemy, the original meaning of the expression in his Aramaic language was *"do not become like"* the opponent. Jesus knew that when we push back against something we feed the power of the attacker and come to reflect it, but when we withdraw from it we build our own force.

That is, while Action-Reaction is the formula of the slave, Action-Maneuver is way of the learned warrior.

Finally, while the art of mastering the War of Maneuver can only derive from long experience and much trial and error, every movement you make in the face of your larger opponent is always seeking out one thing: the critical opening and the decisive thrust that will devastate your adversary.

Your maneuvers, in short, must ultimately be offensively oriented and not be simply a flight from conflict or from direct confrontation with your adversary. For such a fight cannot be avoided. At the same time, all of your methods when dealing with your adversary must be flexible and change in the light of your experience of what works and what doesn't.

In Sun Tzu's words, *"Successful maneuvers are the offspring of true experience but must always remain supple and expendable. Maneuvers are by their nature transitory; if they are enshrined into a permanent strategy or doctrine, they are a recipe for disaster. Every operation must be geared to the rapid seizure and exploitation of the key moment of opportunity created in battle, which can never be predicted. The purpose of every maneuver is to recognize and act decisively upon such fleeting moments to gain an offensive advantage."*

No maneuver against your opponent can have any chance of success without a knowledge of the nature and movements of your adversary. You must know him in all his facets.

Chapter Three: Knowing Your Adversary

Knowing the enemy and knowing yourself: in every battle, no danger. Not knowing the enemy and knowing yourself: one defeat for every victory. Not knowing the enemy and not knowing yourself: in every battle, certain defeat. - Sun Tzu, **The Art of War**

True knowledge of the enemy comes only from active contact with him. - Sun Tzu, *ibid*

Evil is Real, Specific and has an Address: People and Institutions of the Lie

A Russian saying goes that everyone reacts differently to a tickle, but always the same to a hot burning iron. Evil is like that. We all may have our own different idea of what evil is in the abstract, but when face to face with it, we all know evil for exactly what it is: an intentional, hideous, undeterred force of corruption and destruction.

Evil is familiar to us, being so common place in our world that we have acclimatized ourselves to it. That existential fact is a constant problem for the truth teller and the prophet. For the cruel injustices and sufferings that give you so many sleepless nights do not disturb the mass of humanity, especially since their rulers and laws expect them to live alongside evil and uphold it.

If evil was a purely individual phenomena, as the exorcism-genre films would have you believe, then dealing with it would be straightforward: you simply exorcise the demon out of some poor helpless kid or drive a stake through Dracula's heart. Things are not so simple.

Unfortunately, evil is intrinsic to creation and mankind, and therefore embodies itself within institutions and entire cultures as "civilization" evolves into ever-increasing complexity. And the ideal system for evil to dwell within and prosper is the Corporation.

The corporate structure is pre-adapted and designed to foster and inflame evil, and normalize it throughout the world. Its hierarchical structure allows evil to be concentrated at the commanding heights of its system and from there percolate smoothly to all of its levels. The compartmentalized culture and mindset of corporate employees prevents evil from being detected or opposed. The vicarious transfer of all moral judgment and capacity to think for oneself from employees to a "higher authority" that is normative in the corporation prevents compassion, values or moral outrage from impeding evil at any level of the system.

In general, the only two stable values of the corporation – the imperative of maximum efficiency and self-perpetuation – provide the perfect medium in which evil can so grow and multiply that it quickly becomes synonymous with the corporation itself.

The proof of all this is found in practice. It is evident in the automatic ease by which even ostensibly "moral" or religious corporations like the Church of Rome can routinely murder, rape and traffic children, commit crime and operate with total impunity and immunity without any semblance of cognitive dissonance by its members. *That is, nobody in the murderous system is bothered by the murder going on because they do not consider it to be a crime.*

This understanding is imperative for any truth teller who does battle with a corporate system, where every normal human value is inverted and subverted to the needs of the corporation.

Evil is falsehood incarnate. Jesus identified this when he declared , *"For the Devil is a Lie and the father of Lies, having no truth within him."* Defying the Natural Law of Truth which is expressed in a normal equality and harmony between all the parts of creation, Evil twists reality into falsehood to corrupt and destroy that Law. Corporations, cultures and individuals can come to embody and reflect such falsehood at every level of their being once evil has assimilated them, and they become People and Institutions of the Lie.

In one sense, individual people of the Lie are easier to identify than an entire organization fueled by falsehood. Such people are functional psychopaths lacking any moral correction in their behavior, and yet who exhibit all the outward signs of morality. They offer empty smiles but feel nothing. A classic example are Catholic church members who keep placing their tithes in the Sunday collection plate even when they know their money will fund a convicted criminal body that traffics children and launders Mafia revenue. These parishioners are dissociated from their own ethics: a huge and seemingly unbreachable disconnect exists between their thoughts and actions.

At a corporate level, such a disconnect is absolute. Truth is simply a tool that serves the collectivity, and your adversary is no different. You will encounter that fact in a big way once your own actions bring down the wrath of your former employer upon you.

The adversary's official account of you and the wrongs you expose will vary according to their need to buttress their own version of events and castigate yours. Their lawyers and spin doctors will continually "move the goalposts" of reality to portray you as a chronic malcontent, or incompetent, or crazy. As we have noted, such misrepresentation makes it essential for you to keep an accurate and daily account of events as a counterweight to their official lies and as evidence in any future litigation.

(Note: A personal journal is normally acceptable as bona-fide evidence of facts in a court of law).

Your tendency when first exposing the enormity of the Lie in your midst will be to try to itemize its every aspect and document each scale of the dragon. In this way, after awhile whistle blowers tend to find themselves unable to see the forest for the trees. The details of what is wrong and what has befallen you will seem crucially important to you but not to the rest of the world.

That is, you must learn to always cut to the essential thing, summarize the problem, and present it in a concise way to those who haven't been through every bloody inch and moment of your ordeal.

Part of the difficulty any truth teller faces when trying to do so is the general "will to disbelieve" that is so entrenched in the citizenry concerning the crimes of the powerful. This is especially the case since the latter are so adept when it comes to concealing their own wrongdoing, relying on the peoples' disbelief that the commanding heights of society can constitute a criminal enterprise.

Subjugated people are conditioned to believe in the virtue of those who rule them: the Big Lie that those with wealth and power deserve it, and know better than we do about the law, and justice, and morality. "Joe Blow" is taught to equate crime with anyone but Prime Ministers, Popes and "leaders", even when such elites continually defraud, rape, murder and steal their way around the planet.

Unfortunately, an equal barrier to stopping the crimes of the powerful lies with the truth teller himself, who so often believes – at least at first – that simply educating the public about such official wrongdoing will cause things to change.

"Education" is not really the issue, nor is it even possible, when none of us are able to truly grasp the problem in the first place: namely, the depth to which institutionalized lies and crimes are entrenched from the highest to the lowest in our culture.

Even after we have seen the enormity of the evidence for ourselves, we tend to hold out a naive hope that one part of a criminal system will reform or mend the other, nasty part. And so some part of us needs to believe that the truth itself, documented and shared widely enough, is capable of opening minds, sparking reform and toppling tyrants.

Perhaps this false and unproven belief is a timid or a lazy rationalization on our part to avoid the inevitable and much riskier task of doing more than "educating" the system about its own wrongs, but of actually bringing to an end what is responsible: namely, the system itself, and all within us and among us that sustains it.

The reason why all of us tend to shrink back from such a revolutionary step isn't ultimately because of fear, but due to our own internalization of the Big Lie that animates whole cultures and institutions. That Lie permeates all of us so thoroughly and hegemonically that it remains invisible to us and is thereby all-controlling. For somewhere in all of us we genuinely believe that "too much" change will cause social disorder and collapse, and therefore has to be avoided; that the system does respond to public pressure and will cure itself; and that gradual and peaceful change is preferable to revolt.

As Saul Alinsky once observed to a group of community organizers in Chicago,

"Anyone can see through a lie, unless he has need of that lie. And everything you've ever been taught about how society runs is a lie that only serves the interests of a wealthy and invisible few. Your job is to help people think, which begins by helping them realize that their own minds have betrayed them because they are not their own, but belong to the minds of other people in which they have been trapped. And people will break out from that trap only by getting kicked in the teeth enough times by the system and having the courage and clarity to learn for themselves what is really going on, and what is really true and false. That's not something that can be taught to them by anything else than their own experience, and the capacity to understand and own that experience."

All of this has great bearing on how you must go about exposing and destabilizing your adversary, be they ever so large.

As an embodiment of the general societal Lie, your opponent operates in a fundamentally different reality from you as one who is committed to the truth of what you have discovered. To your adversary, their lie represents the truth, and you represent a flagrant untruth. You are the problem in their mind: a permanent impediment to be exorcised and destroyed once your "correction" has proven to be impossible.

In the manner of the medieval Vatican Inquisitor, to your adversary, authority can never be wrong: only the "heretic". So at a basic level, you and your opponent have no common language, except the only kind they understand: power.

A perfect case in point is the fact that it was only when the mainline churches of Canada were threatened with major lawsuits by aboriginal survivors of their crimes that the churches came to the bargaining table to discuss reparations. All of the prior moral and justice appeals by the same survivors had for years fallen on the deaf ears and hearts of these corporations, whose ultimate truth and loyalty was and remains their bank accounts. For to quote Saul Alinsky again,

"Only when you've got your enemy by the balls do their hearts and minds follow".

In short, any Big Lie is broken down not by education or enlightenment in the abstract, but by a threat to the power of whatever is that embodies that Lie. Once your adversary realizes that they can suffer and lose their shirts because of you and what you represent, the fragile and self-serving paradigm of untruth that sustains and legitimates their corporation begins to break down. Your job is to make sure it collapses altogether.

Your enemy will fight you to the death, of course; and the chief way they'll do so is through their enormous arsenal of lies, in which they specialize. Their entire corporate culture is trained to snuff out brush fires of truth and justice by so confusing the world about those igniting and fanning the flames that any effort to stop their wrongs is ended before it ever begins.

Once you persist for long in your quest against their monolith, you will be targeted by them for a permanent campaign of character destruction and public erasure that will never stop, even if you do. Short of physically killing you, which is never their preferred solution since it will generate a martyr's halo around your memory, your adversary will seek to achieve something much more effective: your public degradation and ruination. Then their Lie will more likely triumph over your truth, and the Truth.

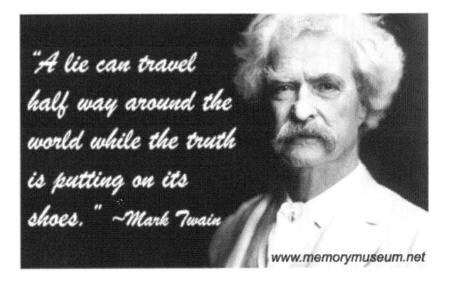

How they will try to achieve your obliteration is a tried and true method as old as the first state power on Earth, and commonly used by governments, churches and any large corporations when faced by people like you. The method is always the same. It involves permanently removing you and your memory from the public mind.

On Being Erased: From Character Assassination to Public Obliteration

A public assault on a man's good name is tantamount to his physical annihilation, for through the assassination of his character he undergoes a kind of social death from which he can never recover. - Judge Louis Brandeis, Justice of the United States Supreme Court, 1923

With his mouth the godless man destroys his neighbor, but through knowledge the righteous will be delivered. - Proverbs 11:9

Fairly early in their assault on you, your adversary will begin to denigrate you within your closest circles, by fabricating lies, half truths and rumors about you to justify their actions against you. They will construct a Straw Man called you, and fill it with every nasty trait imaginable. But if you persist in your stand despite these falsehoods, that kind of defensive denigration will escalate quickly into a more offensive kind designed to permanently blacken and destroy your name to the world and posterity.

The aim of all that, of course, is to erase you from humanity's memory.

Your adversary wants people to be afraid of you. They want you to be mistrusted and not believed, and written off as a nut; even worse, they want the world to consider you to be an immoral and unprincipled lowlife.

In the short term, it will be relatively easy for them to achieve this assassination of your character, especially if you assist their efforts by appearing desperate, angry or prone to rash and unsubstantiated claims. Much of what the adversary does by their smearing of you is designed to get you to over react and step into the debased character portrait they've made of you. *At every step, you must refuse to do so.*

That's easier said than done, naturally, since whenever we're lied about our heart and knee jerk reaction is to get angry and self-defensive, and call other people liars. The genius of a rumor is that it can never be completely refuted, and in trying to do so you become tangled up in angry self-defensiveness, which is what your adversary wants you to be.

Few of us have the discipline or spiritual grounding to receive a vicious blow and not respond in kind. *Nevertheless, you can and should respond to lies said about you, but always from an objective and calm moral high ground.*

Whenever you are attacked with lies and smears, you must always ignore personalisms and stick to the main issue, which is the crimes and wrongdoing of your adversary. Refuse to respond on the terms the adversary has set by not replying tit for tat to their absurd claims; instead, redirect the issue away from you to the adversary. Every lawyer knows that whoever defines and directs the issue before a court will more likely win their case.

The methods used to erase you by your adversary's lawyers and their PR assistants can be boiled down to what we call "The Three D's".

The "Three D's" Method used by your Adversary: Distraction, Discrediting and Destruction

First we fog them, then we blacken them, then we wipe them out. - RCMP Inspector Peter Montague, in reference to aboriginal protestors at Gustafson Lake, BC, 1995

Distraction / Re-directing

In December 1995, one week after I first made Canadian news charging my employer, the United Church, with the death of Indian children, that church publicly announced that I faced "de-listing proceedings" and expulsion from my livelihood as a clergyman. In this way, the church adeptly redirected the issue away from dead Indian kids to my professional standing and by insinuation my veracity and reliability.

Thinking for a moment like your adversary does – and learning to do so is essential as you do battle with them – the first essential thing to do when your wrongs are being exposed is to get people to stop looking at them: to *redirect* their attention to some erroneous issue, and in the process to de-legitimate the claims of the exposer.

Phase One of the adversary's public destruction of you will always consist of such a massive Re-Direction of public attention and discourse away from their crimes. The media will tend to listen to your adversary and accept their interpretation and re-direction. And your job is to constantly redirect things back to their crimes.

The main ingredient of any re-direction campaign is a combination of false or fabricated information and "blind" media reports that create a false narrative about you or the issue raised by you. Lawyers sometimes call this creating a "paper trail" that leads nowhere and confuses and fogs the solid evidence you have unearthed.

For instance, soon after I first released testimonies and documents showing that children had been deliberately killed in United Church Indian schools, the church's head office announced that their own "Task Force" into the same schools had found "no evidence" of any such deaths. The same week, the RCMP – that had worked with the United Church in imprisoning Indian children – also announced their own "Residential Schools Task Force" that – lo and behold! - had similarly found "no evidence of deaths or foul play" in the schools.

Both the church and RCMP accompanied their sudden "reports" with scathing denunciations about me that publicly raised questions about my mental stability.

At that time, it no doubt seemed odd to any intelligent observer that the cops and the church, as the accused, could try to make a neutral claim about their own institutional behavior. And yet a mainstream body like the United Church and RCMP can make public statements without providing any supporting evidence, and they will be generally believed.

Such is not the case with a lone truth teller, like you; for even when you thoroughly document and substantiate your accusations against your big opponent, you will automatically be disbelieved.

The weight of publicly-perceived truth is always on the side of the big battalions – the socially "legitimate" institutions - even if they have blood on their hands. This cruel and unjust fact will be used to the hilt by your adversary to keep you vilified and ignored, and the limelight redirected away from the truth you bear.

At the same time, the weight of hard evidence, accumulated and presented by you over time, can begin to tip public attention and debate away from your adversary's red herrings back to the issue of their crime. This is especially so if you have living eyewitnesses to what you are claiming, so that it isn't just you who is making the allegations against the adversary.

Practical Note No. 6: Learn to use the media and big public events to grab and keep the spotlight. Stage regular press conferences and vigils featuring eyewitnesses, new documents and other evidence that prove your claims. Always look for a an original "hook" to make your material news worthy; DO NOT say what you did the previous week but put a new emphasis on your evidence. Keep pounding away on the issues that keep your adversary on the defensive and reacting to your initiative. That will make it more difficult for them to redirect the issue.

Understand too that the use of language and certain words is key to any strategy of redirection. Your adversary will strive to fog, qualify and minimize any evidence of their crime that you reveal by couching it in"tranquil"or non-criminal expressions. You must counter respond by never fudging your statements but always call a spade a spade: say "murder" when it's murder.

The classic example of this was the Canadian government's use of the tort-related term "abuse" to describe the criminal acts in the Indian residential schools. These places were neither "schools" nor places of "abuse", but of proven torture, rape and murder. But nowhere in the official church and state discourse have these terms ever been used, for they imply criminal and not simply civil actions. In short, in the public mind, actual crimes were reduced to minor tort offenses.

Language is ultimate power, for it frames how reality is perceived and understood. Single catch words and phrases can and do mold public attitudes in an instant, as in "This man is very controversial"or "The alleged misdeeds of the government of Canada".

From Day One, your adversary will use a very directed language to belittle and demean you and your claims in the public eye, and in any court of law. You must therefore use the power of your own words, spoken directly from your heart, to keep things focused on the raw truth of what you have uncovered. *And never, ever, let others speak for you and try to "represent" you and your truth.*

Understand that the Distraction and Re-Direction campaign of your opponent will normally succeed, perhaps for a long time. Your days will be filled with the teeth-grinding outrage of seeing all the wrongs that you have struggled to expose misrepresented and redefined as something not that serious.

You cannot underestimate the psychological burden that will descend on you by living with such a seemingly daily defeat. In some ways it is the hardest load you will have to carry.

Because of this, every day of your life you must recommit yourself anew to what you know is true, and seek to present that truth in new, creative ways to the world. This requires a special kind of will and consecration that while sustaining you will be exhausting, and will cause you to feel estranged and permanently apart from everything and everyone you once relied on. You must therefore learn to pace yourself, and always retain the long term perspective that time is always on the side of the truth.

Imagine the redirection struggle as a perpetual game of ping pong. You must never take your eye off the ball and the new ways your adversary will lob it at you. **Stay alert! And keep directing everything back to what matters.**

Discrediting

The Devil can't put in what isn't already there. - Irish proverb

Knocking down and de-legitimating everything you attempt to do will be the chief aim of your adversary. But they won't be able to succeed in such a discrediting effort without your help.From the start of your long, lonely battle, it will seem like badness is simply being done to poor, innocent you. Rightness will seem to be in your corner, and evil in theirs. That attitude is illusory.

There are no absolute goods and evils in your battle, only shifting power balances. To some degree you are the architect of your present situation, and the outcome is entirely in your hands. You can capitulate at any point and stop your fight. If you refuse to do so, you are handing the enemy the means to further discredit you, by allowing yourself be portrayed as intransigent and inflexible.

To discredit another person is a tricky and unpredictable operation, even for a big corporation. For them to simply call you names leads nowhere, and over time brings more attention to you. To truly discredit a man or woman and what they stand for requires the active participation of the targeted individual in their own demise.

The hard truth is that the moment you choose to go up against a big institution with a truth mostly known only by you, you have already discredited yourself in the eyes of most of the world. *For the onus is now entirely on you to prove your claims beyond any reasonable doubt,* against the overwhelming might and feigned legitimacy of your adversary.

Here is the unavoidable issue: How well can you prove what you claim, with actual evidence and not mere conjecture or opinion? And is the evidence you present verifiable and able to stand up under intense scrutiny and cross examination?

Most of the time, truth tellers lack a lot of such evidence. Their proof of wrongdoing or crime is often experiential or partial: a brief glance at an incriminating letter, an inner foreboding, hearsay or gossip from other people, or a sudden realization of criminality at work that can't necessarily be quantified or demonstrated. None of this by itself is "proof" under legal rules of evidence.

In reality, to make a credible case before any court or inquiry, you need eyewitnesses, experts, and hard data gathered over time to prove beyond a doubt that your employer or some other big actor is actively doing wrong.

Further, even with such evidence you will face the "jigsaw" dilemma of how the different pieces are put together to create a convincing picture. *Correlation, after all, does not indicate causality.* For example, for decades the big asbestos companies won lawsuit after lawsuit brought against them by families of asbestosis victims because the latter were unable to show the specific connection between their fatal illness and specific and intentional acts by the companies. Isolated and probably penniless, you will now face the gargantuan task of somehow doing exactly that: of showing the proof that your adversary is guilty of an intentional and committed crime.

To say that the odds are against you is more than an understatement. This is especially so since the moment you are fired or targeted, all of your access to the evidence that might convict your opponent will normally be cut off to you. Witnesses will be silenced and documents destroyed. Laboring under constant attacks, your main energy will be in defending or justifying yourself and not going on the offensive and gathering new dirt on your enemy. To do all of that takes time, support and money, none of which you will have. The wrongs may be apparent to you, but to very few others. And that will not be enough with which to beat your enemy.

At some point in your battle, depending on the degree of your honesty, you will recognize how little ammunition you actually hold. This realization will cause some of you to despair and perhaps surrender.

Fortunately, we find that most truth tellers who have lasted this long in the fight do not simply collapse. Instead, they try to create new ammunition for themselves where none exists. They are tempted to exaggerate, speculate and make claims that cannot be substantiated, and thereby they hand to their adversary a perfect means to discredit them.

Your main strength as a whistle blower is your truthfulness and integrity; and yet you are one who normally lacks the means to prove what you're claiming. The longer you persist in trying to bring down Goliath with just a few pebbles of truth, the more you will reach for anything to increase your impact and convince the world and posterity that you are right.

Instead of pointing to evidence, you may call upon others to speculate and leap to conclusions you have reached. Your words may assume a religious appeal rather than a delineation of fact. In your zeal and perhaps desperation, you will hope that your own anger at an injustice will take seed in others and have them look past the fact that you may not have a lot of evidence to prove your case. And you may thereby prove your adversary's claim, that you are a shrill conspiracy theorist bearing a personal grudge rather than the truth.

That's the worst case scenario.

Let's say, on the contrary, that you <u>are</u> somehow given the evidence and means to prove your claims, and that you are validated. Do you then really expect justice to "roll down like a mighty river, and righteousness like an everlasting stream"?

I know I did. For I was one of those rare truth tellers who had the fortune to have all of my statements proven by events and many witnesses. Even my adversaries – the churches and government of Canada – were compelled to formally "apologize" for the Indian residential schools they ran, and even admit that thousands of children had died therein.

And then what happened? Nothing. The criminals exonerated themselves publicly, legally indemnified themselves, bought off and silenced the witnesses and left me and my work hanging out to dry. I was proven right, alright, and yet ironically I became even more publicly discredited, ostracized and vilified by the very fact that I <u>was</u> right about something nobody wanted to look at.

All of that proved to me that whatever our battle, it is never consummated, nor does it ultimately boil down to the truth or being proved right.

In our culture, legal "justice" means a financial settlement and nothing more. If you want more than that, and your adversary is big enough, you can never defeat them short of a revolution. They will always be able to outflank, outspend and outfight you, if they want to badly enough; and they will be the ones to write the official history about their own crimes, and about you.

In that sense, you will always be discredited in the eyes of so-called "mainstream" opinion. You will find yourself a permanent exile from all that you knew.

And thank God for it.

The hidden story and purpose of your battle will only emerge after these many defeats, and after all of the adversary's discrediting efforts have run their course and you remain standing with the truth that you now embody. And that's part of the secret of your journey: provided you endure them, all of the attacks and lies thrown at you are actually part of your means to leave one world and enter another one, and thereby gain a power you never had before as a mere victim.

More on that later.

In the short term, there are definite things never to do to avoid being discredited early on in your struggle:

DO NOT make a statement that you can't back up with evidence and proof.

DO NOT engage in name calling, obscenities, personal attacks, or incitements to physical violence.

DO NOT be provoked into angry, impulsive remarks.

DO NOT have anyone else speak on your behalf or speak in the name of your efforts without first approving their remarks.

DO NOT associate with unstable individuals with their own axes to grind, or with dubious, unrelated causes, lest you and your campaign be found guilty by association.

DO NOT accept money or endorsements from people or groups you don't know.

DO NOT walk into obvious set ups or entrapments, especially sexual or financial ones.

In short, don't be stupid.

As your battle proceeds, you must understand that you are no longer free to act with the impunity you once did before being targeted. Calculate everything you say and do, at all times.

Destruction – Their "Final Solution" for you

When all else fails for your adversary and if what you keep doing poses a real threat to their power, they will set out to destroy you for good, including by killing you. That's the easy part for them. Every corporation, government and big private interest in the world have their own hired death squad or third party contractors who are specialized to do exactly that.

Killing an opponent may be easy but it's never the preferred route. Not only does it bring lots of attention on the victim and his claims, but it creates a halo of martyrdom around him and proves to a formerly skeptical world that *"The guy must really have been on to something."* Assassinating a truth teller will often ensure the long term survival of his cause, far more than if he had have simply been left to struggle away in isolation and obscurity.

The truth is that the biggest cause of your destruction will likely not be from a bullet or a bomb, but due to the general indifference of the crowd and your increasing social marginalization.

Time may be your ally in terms of its power to eventually bring out the truth of what you claim; but it is also your worst enemy in terms of your own survival. After a few years if not a few months, what you are struggling to prove will invariably become dead news, repetitive, and of no interest to people, even if it involves horrible crimes and threats to the community. And that by itself can wear down and destroy you.

The preferred method of destruction by your adversary will be relying on such a wear and tear of time, helped along by their character assassination of you to keep any help for you at bay. Killing someone's public reputation is a hundred times more effective than snuffing them out physically, for it imposes a permanent social death on the targeted individual that can never be undone.

I've come to know "survivors" of such social death, and they are all hollow, beaten individuals, and not simply because of their age. One of them who I met forty years ago had endured attacks and blacklisting during the McCarthy era.

Although once a distinguished scholar in Montreal, this man could never get a job, rent a home or establish any permanent group of friends. His name was anathema to everyone he came in contact with, and he was shunned as somebody more dangerous than a leper – even after the McCarthy years had "officially" ended.

In his words, said to me just a year before he died of heart failure,

"I've felt like a walking ghost for over twenty years"

This man faced something more than simple targeting by a private interest: like me, he was in the cross hairs of a modern state, which has the means to neutralize and wipe out not just inconvenient individuals but entire movements for social change. We'll discuss that in the next section.

In terms of your own fate, the daily possibility of your own destruction at the hands of your adversary will hang over you now for the rest of your life. And yet they will never be able to snuff out the truth you have raised and who you are.

In time you may realize that your main job in the long run is to work for posterity and not for simply some short term goals. For in the face of destruction, you have been given a sacred responsibility to share all that you know for the sake of those who, today or tomorrow, will suffer at the hands of what you have exposed.

In that light, here are a few things to remember:

1. Death threats are a normal part of the psychological warfare used by your adversary to get you to shut up or stop. You will be issued them by phone, email, in person or by methods designed to scare the crap out of you. But don't forget, people who make threats aren't normally going to act on them. If they wanted to kill you, they'd simply do it and not give you a warning. After awhile, threats alone simply become boring.

2. Everything and everyone you love will become a target for destruction, if push comes to shove. If you have a family or children you are especially vulnerable, although if you pose a big enough threat you will quickly lose legal custody of your children, rendering you devastated but actually freer to pursue your cause. All things have their light and dark aspects.

3. You must understand yourself well enough to know how you react to losing everything and everyone you loved. In one sense you won't know this until it happens, but grief that

enormous does odd things to people. The greater these stresses, the more you must turn inward to find the inner resources and strength to endure. No-one will be able to do that for you. Learning self-reliance in all things is your primary shield against the threat and reality of destruction.

In the words of Sun Tzu,

"What you love makes you vulnerable. Prepare yourself to relinquish it and you will learn how to conquer death."

State sponsored Disruption - Lessons from COINTELPRO

The FBI's Counter Intelligence Program (COINTELPRO) was begun after World War Two and aimed primarily at disrupting the Communist Party of America. During the 1960's, it was broadened dramatically to infiltrate and destroy domestic political dissident groups, especially among the Black and indigenous populaces. In a few short years, COINTELPRO effectively wiped out the Black Panther Party, the American Indian Movement (AIM), and countless progressive movements, including by isolating and setting up for assassination over one hundred leaders of these groups.

The same methods used by COINTELPRO are now routinely deployed by governments and corporations against their opponents, including infiltration, psychological warfare, harassment and systematic terror and violence.

Lone whistle blowers are relatively easy to isolate and discredit, and so are often spared the full weight of such attacks, which are normally reserved for bigger political movements that pose a collective threat to moneyed vested interests. And yet especially threatening truth tellers are also targeted by COINTELPRO methods, especially if they become publicly and politically prominent and begin to gather support in the media and from beyond their immediate circles.

The first level of a COINTELPRO-style assault involves the infiltration of informants and agents into your work or organization. Informants and Agents are two different types of enemy.

Informants are everyday people recruited and sent in merely to gather evidence. Agents are trained professionals who not only spy on the whistle blower but disrupt their work and discredit them to others. The main way this is done is through the so-called "bad jacketing" method aimed at subverting the reputation of the truth teller and other effective leaders of their movement.

Bad jacketing is character assassination with a vengeance. It involves planting doubts, lies and fabricated evidence that make people believe that any particular leader is in fact a fraud, taking bribes or even working for the other side.

The aim of bad jacketing is not only to discredit and destroy targeted leaders but create a permanent atmosphere of paranoia and mutual distrust among movement members that ultimately destroys that movement from within.

On three separate occasions I have experienced such methods used effectively to destroy groups I had helped establish to expose and confront crimes against humanity in Canada. The pattern and outcome of these disruptions was always the same.

In every case, former supporters of ours suddenly became suspicious and distant without explanation. Scurrilous rumors that could never be traced began to circulate about me and the other spokespeople of our campaign. Fund raisers as well as key witnesses dropped away and facilities became closed to us, always without any explanation. Everyone in our group became seized with such a general confusion and fear that soon our work collapsed.

The first time this occurred, in the summer of 1998 in Vancouver after I had helped convene the first independent Tribunal into residential school crimes, we were able to trace the disruption to two infiltrators who had a past connection with the RCMP. Later, when I de-centralized my work to prevent the repetition of these disruptions, the attacks tended to come more over the internet as part of a permanent misinformation campaign about me and our campaign. But the very unrelenting consistency of these attacks was and remains for me the best confirmation that my truth telling efforts hit some serious nerves and were on the right track.

In other words, you can often tell you're having an impact simply by the level of disruptive attacks being leveled at you. In this way, you can use your adversary's assaults as a sort of barometer to gauge your effectiveness.

All of the COINTELPRO-style methods involve different forms of psychological or physical warfare aimed at you and what you represent. If smears and discrediting campaigns do not stop you, then more forceful methods will be used, including assaults, direct harassment and outright terror.

These direct attacks normally include using the legal system to criminalize you and those who help you. One of the most common ways to do this, especially if you have children, is to ensure that you face divorce and that any subsequent child custody settlement goes against you, and you are then faced with crushing child support payments. Once in arrears of these payments you can be legally imprisoned and lose your passport, and thereafter wear the odious label of a non-supportive, "dead-beat" parent: another arrow in the smear-arsenal of your adversary.

Besides routine harassment from the police, you may also find yourself facing false charges and even wrongful imprisonment over minor incidents. The government may issue false tax claims against you and revoke your driver's license and even passport without cause. All of these are standard COINTELPRO methods designed to make you a criminal under the law.

When the pressure on you is ramped up even higher, your home and office will be broken into and vandalized and your laptops and records will go missing. You may be gang stalked and followed by unknown assailants who bait, harass and attack you without warning. Your movements will be followed by police and unmarked vehicles. All of this is to intimidate you enough so that your free movements and plans are shut down, and you are unable to function normally.

This is nothing less than state terrorism aimed at a targeted individual: you. Notwithstanding this gloomy prognosis, you can overcome the mightiest attacks of the state or any corporate body by understanding its nature and its inherent weaknesses.

The Nature of all Institutional Power and its Achilles Heels

Aristotle said that one must first understand the nature of something to know what it will do. Yet few people, and fewer "activists", bother to know the nature of what they face before trying to engage it, with normally disastrous results.

It is an accurate but glib formality to say that all modern institutions are motivated primarily by the need to keep hold of their power, which means their profits and public image. While true, this barely scratches the real nature of what they are.

Beneath and within the structures of corporate systems lies an energy signal that guides the entire complex. That energy is by nature parasitic and insatiable. It seeks to devour all of creation and humanity and integrate their biomass into itself.

Institutions today are not separate systems but are components of that corporate parasitic entity. There is no such thing as a "private" and a "public" sector, any more than there are lawful courts, accountable politicians or that quaint mental pablum served up for the masses called "democratic process". All of that is window dressing on the global Corporatocracy: a soulless machine that runs every aspect of our world and which you will be confronting head-on the longer you persist in your stand.

Knowing this is not enough. For behind the corporate machine, like with every physical phenomenon, reposes the essential nature of any thing – some call it its spiritual essence – that acts like a directing consciousness or Over Mind. Plato called it the Source. Lazy thinkers say it's God. The philosopher Marcus Aurelius called it the "Hegemonikon" - an overarching intelligence that directs all the thoughts and actions of the inhabitants of any system. This presence exists symbiotically with the people who are part of it, so "hegemonically" that people are not aware of its presence, for its thoughts and impulses are their own.

This Hegemonikon rules its individual parts by governing all habitual rather than conscious thoughts and actions. It establishes a reigning world spirit that directs institutions and nations. It is experienced in an everyday sense as "the way things are". Ultimately it is what keeps humanity trapped in oppressive, enslaved lives and subject to the rule of elites.

To alter that enslavement one must affect the Hegemonikon at its source and not its physical manifestations, like particular institutions, corporations or governments. The roots and not the branches of this thing must be targeted. But how?

As complete as peoples' adherence to the status-quo may appear to be, the actual hold of this hegemonic system of rule by a few over the many is extremely tenuous. Being an energetic hold, it is in constant flux.

The illusion this Hegemony casts is one of power and permanence in order to maintain men and women in the low, controllable mental frequency of fear. But once that mask is pulled back, people begin to awaken from the illusion and realize that they have control over their own energy signal. They can withdraw that energy from the Hegemonikon and establish their own system of self-consciousness and power. And then the Corporatocracy begins to falter.

I have witnessed this happen in the course of our campaign that dislodged "Pope Benedict" from power early in 2013.* *(see below)* Put simply, when people awaken to the real, murderous nature of what they belong to, their mental and then complete withdrawal from it actually starts to decompose and disestablish even the strongest hegemonic system from within. Once a critical mass of such non-cooperation is reached, systems collapse and revolutions occur, provided that enough people are able to create a working alternative to the old regime.

… ....

* *The entire account is found in my book <u>Unrelenting: Between Sodom and Zion</u> (2016, Amazon.com)*

All of that is a long way of addressing how we as truth tellers go about confronting, fighting and stopping a criminal Corporatocracy, and specifically the thing that has targeted us. We do so with our inner eyes open and our minds separated from our former habitual assumptions and ways of thinking. None of that happens overnight. Experience and honest reflection will provide you with the inner road map to navigate and engage with the thing that you are actually confronting.

We have described the essential nature of that thing. How it manifests in an everyday sense is much more obvious: as seemingly immovable corporate hierarchies that are trying to denigrate and destroy you and what is to them your dangerous truth. If our energetic and mental withdrawal from the spirit that animates these corporations is its essential Achilles Heel, its even more immediate point of weakness lies in its inability to maneuver and respond to whatever you do.

In short, you can continually outflank your corporate adversary because of its very power and size.

In 480 BC the much smaller Greek navy outfought and destroyed an enormous Persian invasion fleet in the Bay of Salamis near Athens. The Greek Admiral Themistocles ambushed the bulky Persian ships and then drove his small Greek triremes close in among the Persians, a maneuever that nullified the Persians' superior firepower while using their bulk to tangle them in confusion. By analogy, that is precisely how we are to attack our corporate adversary: up close, aggressively, and unpredictably, so as to allow their own superior fire power to destroy themselves.

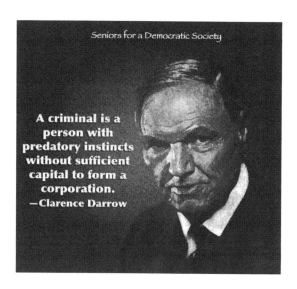

Seniors for a Democratic Society

A criminal is a person with predatory instincts without sufficient capital to form a corporation.
—Clarence Darrow

That is, when confronting a bigger opponent we can goad them into actions that expose themselves and lead to their demise. For don't forget: your adversary has everything to lose, and all that they do is obsessively oriented to protecting what they have at all costs. What a marvelously vulnerable position! How easy it is to provoke and direct such an enemy!

The power-obsessed nature of institutions can also be relied upon if you bother to go the route of negotiations with your adversary. They will be using an enormous hammer to try to squash a little buzzing fly – you – to death. They will keep missing, provided you don't keep flying in straight, predictable lines. And soon they will tire of swinging at you and become desperate, angry and careless. That is when you should strike back at them: when they are off balance.

In the final analysis, institutions are governed not by passion but protocol, and that rigidity makes them a bigger and more vulnerable target than you. Our strengths of compassion, integrity, will and courage have shown to be stronger than any machine, provided they are given the freedom to be.

Chapter Four: Surviving Your Adversary

Invincibility lies in the defense, the possibility of victory in the attack. But supreme excellence consists of breaking the enemy's resistance without fighting. - Sun Tzu

Your best teacher is your last mistake. - Ralph Nader

The first time I ever engaged in paint ball warfare I was fifty eight years old, and I won the battle against much younger and more seasoned opponents. My secret? While the others raced for an advantageous position or immediately started shooting and thereby exposing themselves, I found a hidden spot behind a covered grove of trees and holed up, waiting and watching. Only when I saw what everyone was doing did I take the occasional shot, but only when I knew I could hit a guy without being seen. Whenever I shot, I crouched down and hid myself, or I relocated to a similarly unseen position. Eventually everyone had wiped each other out and I emerged victorious.

To win that day, as I have done throughout all of my public campaigns, I used a strategic defense in the manner of any guerrilla fighter up against heavy odds. Such is the general strategy of the truth teller in relation to their corporate adversary.

Finding and Holding the High Ground

Every guerrilla fighter must ask himself, how do I survive an enormously powerful adversary while continuing to engage them? How do I maximize my advantages and minimize theirs? How do I maintain my firing position and keep them on the defensive without exposing my position?

The answer to all of these and other problems facing a small force is the same: you must find a secure high ground position and hold it flexibly, preparing to relocate at any moment along secure fall back routes.

Morally, physically and publicly, the truth teller must always seize and hold the high ground from where he can dominate the field of battle. The face of war shows us time and again that a tiny, well- entrenched and supplied force on a high ground position can hold out against a huge army indefinitely while inflicting disproportionately greater injuries on the attacker.

The moment you choose to combat an evil and those responsible, you must define and retain not only the moral high ground but the issue as a whole. You must command the battle by defining the ground: the issues and the facts of your case. If you let your adversary do so you have already lost the war.

To define your battle should be straight forward for you, since you know the issues backward and forward. But you have to summarize what is obvious to you and present it to the world and your supporters so that they know what the battle is about and what it is you want.

To affect this, prepare a written and video statement about everything and blast it out to the media the day you are fired or first attacked. Dominate the news by original and damning evidence and audacious public acts that catch peoples' imaginations and secure your position on the moral and informational high ground.

As in any battle, once you have achieved this advantageous position your enemy will try to drive you from such security by forcing or luring you off it. They will attempt to lull you with talk of negotiation and compromise in order to buy time to finish you off. That's the general purpose of their lawyers: to either scare you or fool you into abandoning your position and then be wiped out.

You must always avoid the impulse to counter attack or come down from your concealed position to enter into "dialogue" with your opponent. That is all a ruse. If the adversary wanted to be reasonable they wouldn't have forced you into battle.

One of the more common errors of untried whistle blowers is to abandon their own high ground position by striking prematurely at the enemy. Excited by new evidence or witnesses that they assume will "prove" the guilt of their adversary before some hypothetically just court of law, the truth teller quickly goes public with it and reveals his sources, aims and strategy prematurely to the enemy. That's precisely what the adversary wants, for they then know how to deal with you and sabotage your actions.

On the contrary, you must learn a deep patience in your high ground position and gather your punch for precisely the right moment from behind a perpetual fog of concealment. When that moment to strike will arrive is impossible to judge before hand; it requires constant observation and reconnaissance-based analysis of the enemy. But especially for a small guerrilla force like yours, timing is everything. Do not fall for the deceptions of the enemy, who will fear your commanding position and seek to pierce your defenses.

The Traps of Negotiation and Compromise

When a bigger opponent claims they want to "negotiate" they are acting either from desperation or deception. Normally it's the latter.

Your institutional adversary is never interested in listening to a trouble maker like you, or working out a "compromise" that benefits both of you. That's only how parties of equal strength think. Your enemy views you as an insignificant upstart who, while possessing potentially damaging evidence on them, simply needs to be brought down and made to comply. That is their sole purpose in "negotiating" with you.

If you're a congenitally trusting or naive individual, you'll last as long in this battle as a snowball in hell. The truth tellers who tend to weather this phase of the battle the best are by nature suspicious and pessimistic people when it comes to the world, and they have usually overcome the infantile need to please an authority figure that can hobble the best of us.

If you do choose to attend a negotiating session with your adversary on their terms, you'll be made to feel instantly small and worthless: by the surroundings, the presence of a battery of lawyers and assorted goons, and the ultimatums placed upon you. That's why you should be the one to establish the place and ground rules of your meeting at the outset.

Before the meeting, insist on convening in a poor or unfamiliar neighborhood where you can bring lots of friends and sympathetic witnesses. That alone will disorient your adversary and put them off their game.

I remember a similar, quite funny moment soon after I was unlawfully fired by the United Church in early 1995.

The church bureaucrats insisted on a meeting to lay out their demands on me, so I said I could only meet in a room at the Christian seminary I'd attended. No doubt made confident and unsuspecting by the choice of the venue, the five church guys showed up that day only to be met by me and a dozen aboriginal people sitting across from them at the head of a long table. They church guys visibly blanched at the sight of all the Indians in the room and hesitated before warily sitting down in front of us. They were so upset they could barely speak; their flaunted power over me had dissipated like a fart.

When the church guys tried to issue their demands on me, I broke in quickly and asked them under what authority were they violating my human rights and due process of law by asking me to agree to my own self-destruction. At that point the once-austere church officers disintegrated into a batch of yelling children, unleashing all their pent up rage at me for spilling their family secret of murdered native children. One of them actually lunged at me across the table as I calmly sat and held an eagle feather. My adversaries not only lost their cool but any control they might have had over the situation. We kept the high ground and they went away depleted and defeated.

That's what I call successful negotiating on the terms of the underdog. An unsuccessful scenario would have been if I had have gone alone to the church offices, sat quietly and respectfully while they read out their demands on me, and then been shut down whenever I tried to speak. For everything is about who keeps the energetic high ground; and who goes away empty.

On another occasion, when the RCMP gruffly demanded that I report to them and answer questions about my allegation of their murder of aboriginal street people in Vancouver, I agreed to see them, but at the community radio station on the next episode of my news program, *Hidden from History*.

"I have questions to ask you guys, too, over the air" I said to the RCMP officer. "Like why you're not being prosecuted for helping to transport and kill children in the Indian residential schools".

That was the last time I ever heard from the RCMP.

Does your enemy want to negotiate and talk? Great. Do so, but always publicly, with lots of witnesses and _always on your terms_. Use the opportunity as a big court of public opinion to expose the adversary and turn the tables on them.

At the end of the day, any initiative by your enemy should be turned back on them, which is easy enough to do, considering the degree of their guilt and liability.

Learning to Be Alone, and Finding your New Family

One of the habitual illusions that even the most hardened truthers experience is the lingering belief that one day the world will rally to the truth and they will be vindicated and welcomed back in from the cold. The truth is bitterly different.

In practice, whistle blowers invariably end up in a form of permanent exile from their former life. Learning to be alone to that degree is never easy for most of us, since we have been taught to look for some ultimate affirmation from society as a whole.

Frankly, you can forget about that ever happening once you go up against powerful enemies.

On the other hand, new life always emerges from the ashes of before. In the course of your long struggles you will encounter a new kind of family: people much like you, but often so hardened by their long night that they are unable any longer to reach out and find a community of like souls. People you never suspect will also appear from out of nowhere to offer you help and support. In these small ways will you learn to endure.

Despite any amount of attacks or troubles that may come your way, it is up to you to keep your own flag flying high for the sake of those unknown friends out there who are silently wishing you well and onwards. We never know who we are influencing, or to what degree. We are planting seeds of thought and action that may take years to blossom in another generation, and that we may never see. We must learn to trust in such a silent growth and elusive springtime.

Part of surviving your long exile involves learning to cherish and draw strength from the small and genuine moments of peace and happiness you can still know. Avoid being cooped up in a small apartment or a heavily urban environment. Stay outdoors and allow mother earth and her energy take your pain and strengthen your center. Be around animals and children. And remember that life and you are so much more than your loss, and the brutality you have come to know.

An essential part of your mental health and inner stability means learning how to pace yourself mentally and emotionally. That is normally a tall request for people as zealous and driven as you and me. And yet however possible, avoid becoming encumbered by the injustices and horrors that you have come to learn. You can stay consecrated to a goal without becoming overwhelmed by it.

The fact is that a wise commander does not engage directly and on the front lines with the enemy but keeps his distance so as to never lose perspective and the general overview by which his force will triumph. If you are depleted and confused your battles will all be lost.

Not many other people can understand your situation or be able to really help you carry your burden. But however possible you need to build some kind of support network around you, even if it is tenuous and occasional. Your adversary will do their best to isolate you completely. You must continually maneuver around their plan.

Ultimately, the longer you endure the stronger you will become, provided you learn the skills of living as a hunted guerrilla leader.

Surviving Underground: Income and Outcome

"So how have you survived economically all these years, with all the blacklisting and attacks you've faced?"

Not a week goes by that someone doesn't ask me that question. It is a fair query. One of your biggest challenges after your firing and blacklisting will be to simply survive materially. Where does the money come from?

Frankly, it *doesn't* a lot of the time. Unless you have a wealthy patron or a relative who doesn't mind being made guilty by association with you, your savings will dry up and poverty and homelessness will quickly loom before you.

The hard reality you will face is that all of the previous guarantees and economic safety valves in your life will be rapidly turned off, one by one. Your adversary will make sure of that.

In just one month, for instance, I faced eviction, permanent unemployment and unemployability, the seizure of my goods and a bill for colossal custody and alimony payments from the church-orchestrated divorce proceedings that stripped me of my children. I literally lost everything, in a material and familial sense.

Such a stripping produces a profound shock within us, as it is meant to do; exactly like the effect of being pounced on and kicked over and over by a gang of attackers. We are permanently disoriented for a time and cannot see anything but our pain. That is normally the time when your adversary will turn up the heat on you and use your shocked condition to force you to capitulate to them, with threats of lawsuits and so on. That is why it is crucial that in response you find some form of retreat - even a room in a friend's house - that nobody knows about and where you can find some semblance of refuge from the sudden storm, if only to get your mind clearer.

Soon enough you will have to face a very ingrained fear you may not have known was in you, especially if you're from an upper or middle class background: namely, the terror of having nothing ... no money, no home, nothing to survive on. This feeling of complete physical vulnerability is a novel fear for many, but not of course for one accustomed to poverty.

Whoever you are, your early phase as a blacklisted truth speaker will tend to consist at first of scrounging a survival for yourself, which of course is part of the adversary's game plan. For if you don't lift your eyes from your own stomach, you can't look ahead and lead any kind of battle for truth.

The only way out of this trap and its fear-manacle is to stop focusing on yourself and worrying about how you'll survive. Think of the countless people who have it much harder than you, and of those who are looking to you to oppose the evil you have exposed. When you learn that the sun no longer revolves around your own life, you can endure incredible hardships and not flinch.

Personally, I found that once I stayed immersed in the struggles of other people I lost a lot of my own disabling pain and self-concern. And in that state of concern-for-the-other, the universe showed me how little I had to worry about when it came to my own survival.

For example, more than once during my early years under the blacklisting, I would end up giving the few dollars I had left to homeless families and those who needed it more than me. Every time, like clock work, money would appear from nowhere that very same day: literally lying on the street or offered to me by a well wisher. I learned something that the birds of the air know, and that Jesus reminded us:

For who of you by worrying can add a single minute to his life? Consider the lilies of the field: they do not toil nor spin, but God in his mercy cares for them. And if God considers these grasses of the fields, which are here today and gone tomorrow, will he not take care of you, his chosen ones, O you of little faith?

Learning such trust is actually part of our evolution out of a false world and back into the natural world and its Law, the recovery of which is part of the purpose of your suffering.

But back to your practical situation. Finding the material means to keep going is ultimately not a personal concern but a political one. You will find the means to survive only by showing other people that you have something important to offer, and are waging a crucial battle for justice and the innocent. Then more support will come to you.

Establishing a constant public and media presence is a key part of this effort. You must stay in the public limelight so consistently that you and your issue become a household word. Donations will then start flowing in to help your work. By the second year of my public campaigning to expose residential school crimes in Vancouver, despite a powerful blacklisting, my appeals for support over the internet and community radio stations were garnering hundreds of dollars from the public to cover my costs for travel, research, leafleting and renting halls for our meetings.

One of the reasons I was able to become economically sustained in my work was because I had a regular platform to broadcast my campaign to the world through a program I started on Vancouver Co-op radio: a program that lasted nine years before being shut down by the government.

That is, as a banned person, you must ultimately rely on yourself and be your own loudspeaker. Nobody is going to hand you a government grant. And you can forget about the corporate or "mainstream" media, especially in Canada. They rarely mention whistle blowers, let alone go to bat for them.

In terms of your daily survival, in reality it doesn't require a lot of money to survive in our culture, if you forgo the comforts and lifestyle you may have grown accustomed to.

Subsidized housing, crashing with friends, and shared apartments are cheap options. Free food and clothing outlets abound in every major city. After my firing I found that I could get by on less than five hundred dollars every month. Of course, I couldn't drive a car – the government had seized my driver's license on a bogus charge, anyway – and public transit tends to increase the daily labor of getting to and fro. But the point is that life is still very doable in a state of poverty once fear is replaced by street smarts.

Again, that's the worst case scenario. Organizing fund raising to provide you with a monthly stipend to carry on your campaign is very doable. Asking supporters for monthly sustaining pledges also works. And the more you fight on for your cause and become known to the world, the more people will pop up out of nowhere to give you a hand. That's a given.

One of the biggest adaptations you'll have to make as a banned and blacklisted man or woman has nothing to do with physical survival, but involve your own expectations of life and your sense of reality.

Before your war, your life and career had definite manageable outcomes. You felt that your present and future could be planned and directed with relative security. None of that is true anymore, once you become a targeted individual. Every day is uncertain, and you seem to have absolutely no guaranteed future.

In your new conditions, you tend to live from moment to moment, and few of your plans ever transpire. You find yourself living in a crisis mode of thinking all the time, waiting any moment for the boot to come down on you again from any direction. Being in such a state quickly constricts your thoughts to "battle mode", as if you're in a forward trench awaiting a massive enemy attack.

That is one of the real outcomes of being a targeted truth teller. There will be very few people with whom you can share your thoughts and feelings. The upside to this condition is that it tends to make you internally self-reliant; the downside is you can become psychologically overwhelmed and driven into incredible despair and regret. Self-pity will be tugging at your psyche a lot, and a deep, burning and inexpressible rage.

These are totally legitimate feelings, and are very human responses to the horrible injustices that have been inflicted on you and others. And the only healthy outcome is to channel such rage and discontent into something greater than yourself: not only your truth campaign but something in the world that you can build and be proud of. Such a sense of accomplishment – that your suffering has been for a tangible purpose that can be seen – is one of the strongest medicines you can prescribe for yourself.

Victor Frankl, the Austrian psychologist who survived Nazi death camps and wrote the book *Man's Search for Meaning*, observed that it was those of his fellow Auschwitz inmates who lacked a daily purpose who died the quickest. Contrarily, the ones who found meaning beyond the unendurable starvation and torture they were experiencing survived the longest.

That meaning was different for each man and woman, but it always involved one of three things, according to Frankl: an intense love, or a commitment to a higher cause, or a creative project. The common denominator of all three was that a higher meaning was found beyond their own life situation.

Once even the most tortured soul finds such a transcendental purpose they acquire a power that can stand up to the worst tyranny and endure any ordeal. By losing their fear of death, they discover the secret of their life. As a targeted truth teller, you are one of those rare and chosen souls who has been given the chance to attain that power, for the sake of justice and humanity.

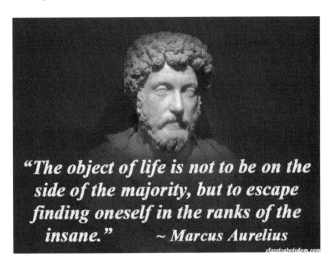

"The object of life is not to be on the side of the majority, but to escape finding oneself in the ranks of the insane." ~ Marcus Aurelius

The Power You Hold: Bringing Down Goliath

For the true man, adversity is his golden time. - John Adams

I felt the cleansing hand of angels on my soul as burning tongs from hell, not knowing that they were actually setting me free. - Meister Eckhardt

Before your war and your loss, you never really knew your own nature. You probably saw yourself as "just another person" who had no intrinsic power or authority, and certainly not enough to challenge the so-called "powers that be". You never had to question that self-conception because it seemed to serve you: when you played by the rules, deferred to another authority, and crept along as a dutiful, subordinate and anonymous person, you seemed to get by.

In an instant, all of that has been shattered. What used to help you is suddenly out to destroy you.

Suddenly, almost overnight, you are no longer anonymous, but the subject of unceasing and cruel assaults by a power that is unrestrained by the law or by any of the authorities you once trusted. You find yourself treated like a leper, shut out and hated for no reason. People fear you.

In a phrase, it's sink or swim time – because the ship has foundered, and there's nobody coming to rescue you.

When I was seven years old, my swimming instructor actually tossed me into the deep end of the pool and then kept shoving me away from safety with a long pole. After my initial panic and unanswered cries for help, some deeper instinct took over inside me and I found myself swimming. That impulse switched on without any effort by me. A desperate situation evoked it.

The hand of fate is like that merciless swimming instructor with the long pole. It keeps shoving us away from an easy recovery and the safety that changes nothing.

As a targeted truther, you have been thrown out in the deep waters to not only learn how to swim, away from the old safeguards, but become a different being in the process. You are being prepared for something greater.

That something isn't too hard to perceive. It stands before you now like Goliath, seemingly triumphant, dripping with blood and challenging humanity to defeat it. And as everyone else around you flees from its terrible power, something in that new, emerging you stands up quietly, and armed by a new faith, steps forward to confront the giant.

That is part of the deeper saga that you have entered. You have been set aside to do the hardest job a human being can do: to expose and bring down institutionalized evil. But much of your old persona must fall away before you are able to step into that new destiny. Your present suffering is the fire that is refining and forging that new and stronger being within you and preparing you for what comes next.

Once you have passed through those flames, you will share no common language with the people around you. They will marvel, from a safe distance, your capacity to endure and to keep fighting the adversary, but they will never understand how you continue. Such people may encourage you in your battle but they will never stand with you, for they remain what you once were: fear-driven men and women raised in slavery. They will constantly remind you that you have entered a new reality in which you stand alone in an arena facing Goliath.

That prospect may have scared you once, but your old fears and impulses are diminishing. What matters now is no longer yourself but the need to strike the decisive blow against your adversary.

Having matured from your loss and trials, you are much better equipped now to strike that blow, and your enemy knows it. Their reactions to you will become increasingly desperate. Unable to hit you directly because of a new radiance and power that surrounds you, they will target those around you and rely on an even greater deluge of lies and misinformation to distract you from delivering the death thrust. Their end is approaching and they know it.

Experience shows that if a truth teller survives the various stages of assault, siege, psychological warfare and perpetual exile, time builds rather than diminishes his and her ability to affect change. The once lone whistle blower transforms into a veteran who poses a fundamental threat to not just his adversary but the entire murderous status-quo that backs them.

That threat is not only because of the knowledge, experience and battle savvy of the truther but the inter-generational inspiration he and she can be to future freedom fighters.

The adversary fears the spreading of the example and the message of the successful truther. Our job is to make sure that it does spread.

Chapter Five: Transformation, Recovery and Victory?

I used to be a victim. Now I'm a threat. - Canadian genocide survivor Harriett Nahanee, 1999

The seeker of truth who journeys long enough becomes the path. - Persian proverb

The fight that ended your old life and birthed a new one is but a single atom in a sick and dying body politic; one battle in an unending war of tyranny against the human race. Early in that battle you no doubt learned that what you faced wouldn't end or be resolved by a glib "apology" from your adversary and a few dollars of reparations. What you experienced has changed your understanding of the world and the psychopaths who run it, and set your face against all of it. It has left you profoundly changed.

In many cultural traditions, the mythic hero is one who is chosen before his birth to endure unspeakable suffering in battle and be exiled from his people by forces of darkness. Only after many years and sorrows does he return to his homeland to find it and himself forever altered.

The real story is that the hero carries within his anguished heart a secret for his people without which they will perish. The hero becomes the bearer of a new world and the midwife of a nation's tomorrow, even though his sacrifice has been made for those who have no ears or eyes to receive the priceless gift he has borne at the cost of everything.

The truth teller is such a hero, and carries a sacred responsibility that few others will bear. But his greatest aspect is revealed as he ages into a battle worn veteran.

As such, the truther is one who has found his purpose, as a light bearer and sage for those who are to follow after him. The truther will never recover his old life nor what has been stripped from him and lost over many struggles; but his greater gain is that he has been transformed into something more essential. He has won not healing, but transcendence, and the victory of having endured and become more than who he once was.

The Great Shift: Becoming and Remaining a Veteran and a Mentor

A veteran knows the score, only too well. Before anything, he is a raw realist, utterly familiar with the underbelly of the Beast. The challenge is to share that score with novices who face an impending big boot. That can indeed be a challenge, from both ends: the veteran truth teller finds little common ground or language with those who haven't experienced what he has, while those new to the struggle naively tend to look for quick and simple remedies without understanding the immensity of the forces that they are up against.

Things aren't helped by the fact that veteran truthers have learned to work and exist alone, and they tend to be tough individualists with stubborn egos who don't have the patience to spoon feed to others the bleak reality of struggling as a targeted man or woman. *"I can't teach you, only experience can"* is one of their more common refrains: something that budding new activists, who are generally wary of "experts" telling them what to do and how to do it, tend to agree with wholeheartedly.

And so in general, the nice idea of veterans mentoring a new generation of whistle blowers doesn't tend to manifest very much in practice, from my experience. The rich and invaluable lessons gained by going through the fire tend not to become shared and generalized, causing the same errors and trials to be repeated over again by each new generation.

Nevertheless, the most crucial outcome of the truth teller's long struggle is to use their knowledge and accomplishments to build up a permanent Army of Truth that can assist and connect up whistle blowers and all freedom fighters early on in their struggles.

Simply listening to the developmental story of a veteran truther's battles is an enormously instructive mentoring that can highlight the many pitfalls, mistakes and illusions to be avoided. Many vital tactics and methods in dealing with powerful adversaries need to be shared and hashed out with newcomers to show them the reality they will face, and assist them to survive and overcome it. Power elites tend to be more alike than different in their reaction to the exposure of their misdeeds; a fact that compels truthers to learn to generalize their experiences and thereby unite and strengthen their separate campaigns.

The ultimate goal is to build a grassroots global movement to deconstruct and de-corporatize the world's power systems, returning that power and its wealth to all the people – provided that the latter are conscious and virtuous enough to receive it. Sparking that flame in the people is part of the job of the veteran truth warrior: an explicitly political and revolutionary task that requires whistle blowers to evolve beyond their traditional "me" focus to one of "we".

Reaching Out and Building Up the Army of Truth

An army of principles will penetrate where an army of soldiers cannot. For such is the irresistible nature of truth that all it asks, and all it wants, is the liberty of appearing. - Thomas Paine, **Common Sense**

An army is built and sustained by the example of its commanders; by actions and not by words. - Sun Tzu

The life of man upon the earth is a warfare, according to the Biblical character of Job, who had cause enough to think so.

Job's experience didn't lie, if you believe the Bible: stripped senselessly of everything by a brutal and unseen power, Job had to make sense of his devastated life while under fire, just like any truth teller does. And like Job, the truther is beset by a chorus of accusers and adversaries determined to plague and distract him from the truth that his agony is revealing. For that truth can one day elevate him past his personal suffering to the purpose Fate has given him, within which he discovers his real power and identity.

As I wrote in a letter to a well wisher after many years of struggle,

"Once I learned why I was being so targeted all of the garbage thrown at me finally made sense. The whole system stood naked and clear to me for the first time in my life. I saw that it was a bloody murderous thing that had to be fought at every level and brought down if any of us were to survive. When I gained that clarity I was never afraid of anything anymore. I'd found my purpose."

The power of a truth teller who endures his ordeal and transforms from victim to warrior is that he finally knows himself to be part of a bigger and normally unseen army that has waged an unending war against tyranny on earth and in heaven ever since mankind's inception. It is a spiritual army but one very rooted in worldly realities and our human struggles. And like any army it operates according to the rules of war.

The Chinese General Sun Tzu, whose wisdom and experience guide this Manual, summed up the rules and principles of warfare in his three broad maxims concerning Leadership, Strategy and Tactics:

1. *Wars are won only when a unified leadership transforms random events into controlled outcomes, by purposely shaping such events. The clarity and will of the commander forms the ground of the entire army; and such clarity comes from honesty and realism. An unshakeable will to pursue victory using every opportunity is the one essential quality of commanders, and overcomes every setback or unforeseen event.*

2. *One skilled in battle summons one's enemy and is not summoned by them; one skilled forms the ground of battle, and the enemy must follow; offers, and the enemy must take. And yet always be invisible and unfathomable to your enemy, and always unpredictable. Use the extraordinary moment to win victory.*

3. *Do not confront the enemy in their strength, but at the points of their weakness. In all engagements, aim at and seize quickly whatever the enemy holds dear; then their strength and plans are rendered useless, and they must stop and respond on your terms. Likewise, whatever you love makes you vulnerable and prone to manipulation: prepare yourself to relinquish it.*

Sun Tzu's detailed insights are found in Appendix Two of this Manual, and they seem tailor-made to small groups engaged against much more powerful adversaries. In that sense, the General's entire outlook should be taken to heart and utilized by any truther. But the preceding three broad maxims uniquely address our situation as we set out to build our Army of Truth.

First Maxim, on Leadership: Despite his own war experience and veteran-like wisdom, a truth teller can remain for too long strangely unconscious of his own leadership purpose, even when a broader movement grows up around him and his issue. Such ignorance is fatal, since who else but a battle-hardened truther can provide the leadership to "transform random events into controlled outcomes".

The adversary has a very clear sense of their own leadership and chain of command, whereas truthers tend to have an individualistic and libertarian attitude to such command. As a result, our forces are normally at a terrible tactical disadvantage in any serious battle, and we usually lose. The first corrective to this is for us to shed our anti-authoritarian bias and recognize that in the war in which we are increasingly immersed, we must constitute ourselves as a consciously-organized and disciplined leadership of the movement around us, and pursue victory to the very end.

Second Maxim, on Strategy: Flowing from this leadership imperative is the understanding that all wars are won by our consciously shaping the ground of each battle, and thereby summoning the enemy to us on our terms while fogging that enemy to our real movements. Only then can we position the enemy to receive our decisive, extraordinary blow.

In short, we must never drift or follow the flow established by our adversary. We must define the issues and movement of any campaign and retain the initiative at all times. Again, only our own self-conscious leadership command can achieve this.

Third Maxim, on Tactics: Similarly, maneuvering to strike a larger opponent at their weak points and where they are most vulnerable requires that the same unified command have both a clear awareness of the enemy and the field of battle, and the capacity to react quickly to shifting events and opportunities. That same leadership - you - must also understand your own vulnerability and relinquish everything that makes you so. This is the hard part of being a commander and not simply an activist.

These considerations highlight a very real and human dilemma for any truther who graduates into the ranks of leadership of a movement: the need to suspend the priorities of a so-called "normal" life because of the requirements of war.

Many of us find it impossible to do this all the way. We have already been stripped of so much of our former life that we have become hardened and used to loss; and yet paradoxically that very denuding makes us want to hang on all that more to at least some shred of an everyday life: a happy relationship, children, financial security. These longings make us especially vulnerable and are a major gap in our armor that the adversary knows how to instantly exploit, to the ruin of not only us but the movement that depends on us.

In short, you must learn to remain alone if you are to lead your army: self-reliant, strong and eternally vigilant.

You will be surprised how naturally you will find this power once you let go of the tendency to keep gazing back with regret or longing at the life you once knew, and which has died. Remain a hard realist without relinquishing your heart.

If you remain in such a public leadership stance, your personal example will draw other veterans to you and your army will grow. You will inspire numbers far greater than you realize, discovering that your greatest weapon against a seemingly overwhelming adversary has always been yourself and your own public example.

The Truth is Your Real Therapy: Beyond Recovery

Occupying that church with all of you and sticking it to those fucking priests did more for me than twenty years of counseling. I'm not afraid of those bastards anymore. - Canadian Genocide survivor William Combes, 2008

Therapy, from the Greek therapeia, "to lift the burden from another" - **Strong's Concordance**

In one sense, it is not possible for a whistle blower to ever "recover" and return to that nebulous notion called a "normal life". The world makes no sense anymore to those like us, and all the old reference points are gone. Like any trauma survivor, a victimized truth teller must take seriously his experience and create his own meaning and health.

On top of this challenge is the fact that in a narcissistic culture like our own, medical "healing" practices are in practice an elaborate form of denial. Personal recovery from any trauma or injustice is narrowly approached as a completely self-centered process of prolonged "analysis".

The aim of such "therapy" is to somehow restore one's previous, status-quo existence. Yet the cause of the trauma is never addressed, and the traumatized one is encouraged to "forgive and forget" the cause and its perpetrator, thereby closing off any chance to deal with normal feelings of outrage, let alone find any justice or resolution. In truth such "therapy" is designed to keep the victim in an unresolved state of trauma and dependency, like any twelve-step adherent, unable to evolve into a mature and integrated personality.

This model seems tailor-made to the needs of the victimizer rather than the victim, and is a far cry from the original understanding of the word "therapy", and the natural human practices of recovery from which that understanding arose.

"Therapeia" means *"to lift the burden from another"*, referring to both the ailing and those who help them. It is an empathic sense of the interconnectedness of men and women and our capacity to invoke restorative power from within and among ourselves, without mediator or professional helper.

This understanding is really derived from an ancient practice of maintaining a natural harmony among people, relying only on ourselves and our God-given, sovereign abilities.

How do victimized truth tellers recover? By *"knowing who they are, and loving what they know"*. By staying true to their own heart, and not falling into the state of despair and self-destruction visited upon them by their adversary. By fighting back and holding to their truth, and to the truth. And in the process of so enduring, by transforming into an even more courageous and authentic self, the man or woman they were meant to be.

That's the personal aspect. But true *therapeia* is also a collective process of many people lifting burdens, restoring life, and maintaining hope for one another. We find our way back to life together, not as self-absorbed victims but as new men and women.

I have personally witnessed this transformation up close with inwardly-destitute survivors of rape and torture who found their courage again by protesting together at the very seat of power of their church torturers, shouting the truth to the world, and facing down their adversaries. They acted, and proved to the world and to themselves that their souls were still their own.

We look beyond personal recovery to a collective transformation, to finding our higher self as part of a movement to reclaim all that has been taken from us in our unconsciousness. That reclamation is the hidden gem buried deep in the traumatic and epic journey of the truth teller who stays on his purpose.

A Final Reckoning?

After a lifetime of this work I can't say I've changed the world that much. But at least I never let it change me. - Don Eperson, veteran radical and hell raiser, to the author, 1978

What more do you want, man, from an act of goodness? Is it not enough that you have done something consonant with your own nature – do you now put a price on it? As if the eye demanded a return for seeing, or the feet for walking. Just as these organs were made for their purpose, so man was made to do good: and whenever he does something good or contributes to the common interest, he has done what he is designed for, and inherits his own. - Marcus Aurelius, **Meditations**

The problem for me isn't surviving. The problem is how to relate to the rest of humanity now that my eyes are open. - Vietnam Veteran Darryl Adams, 1981

If you've read this far or even deigned to pick up this Manual, you're not the kind of man or woman to live alongside an evil or rest at half measures.

You wouldn't have defied your employer or some other powerful adversary if you were the kind to go along with the herd or who could be placated with a few dollars and a pat on the head. You live to see justice done; and by that I mean a final justice, so that tyranny and oppression isn't just momentarily paused but eradicated, especially when it tries to crush the weakest among us.

People like us seem like suckers for punishment to the rest of the world. Knowing wrong is at work, we are unable to sleep at night when everybody else can. We are like the Biblical prophets who blasted their own people for their misdeeds, but not in their own name; they spoke as the loudspeaker of Natural Justice. And they lived and died as scorned outcasts.

If there is any ultimate reward for us, it lies only in one quality, really: our capacity to remain ourselves and see our lonely purpose through to the end. So don't expect to ever be vindicated or honored by the rest of the world, or by the people you've fought and died for. And yet that hope will always linger. Being who we are, our hearts can never relinquish the vision that one day the Beast we've fought will be de-fanged, and right will prevail.

That's not the problem for us, as the years pass. As any war veteran encounters, the problem for a truth warrior is relating to the "normal" world now that we see things as they really are. We've left the fairy tale world we were raised in and deal now in the cold hard reality of what is. And this leaves us with a profound disorientation, a sense that we can never belong anywhere, ever again.

In short, we have become exiled from our old existence not just by circumstances and our adversary, but by the fact that we are profoundly different people now. And as such we cannot find any final reckoning unless it is in the company of those who have also made such a shift.

Can the world change with us? Has all our sacrifice done anything to alter the nature of mankind into something better?

Whenever a criminal adversary is caught publicly in their own wrong doing, their public relations experts quickly begin bleating about "reconciliation", which is always the refrain of the guilty. That cheap and self-serving slogan is not what we envision as mankind's final accord with itself. The lion will lie down with the lamb only when there are no longer lions or lambs. Mankind must change its warlike and divided nature if we are to survive ourselves.

Such an ultimate outcome may not rest in our immediate hands, but as truth warriors we hold an invaluable piece of our evolution up from savagery.

Here in our long darkness, we have held up a lamp consisting of our reason and our integrity, and the capacity to not go along with anything that debases the human soul. We have raised up humanity by doing what is right, which, like a single ripple spreading out through space and time, leaves its mark forever on those who will follow after us.

It is said that, near the end of his short but wondrous life, Alexander the Great sat down and wept because there were no more kingdoms left for him to conquer. Your life as a truth teller can seem like that, the older you become. The mountains you have moved by your stand will still loom before you, and the world may seem not that different for all your labors. But you have left your mark.

And with that mark, hopefully you have also gained the wisdom that assures you that others will learn from your example and for years to come will put their own shoulders against the mountains of wrong.

There is indeed a final reckoning between the light and the shadow, and you are a part of it as long as you draw breath. The point is to never yield: to fight and not to count the cost or seek any reward save that of doing what is right and defending the helpless. That is surely the best epitaph of anyone devoted to the truth and to their fellow man and woman.

Appendix One: Doing Research and Investigations

You can't make up in passion what you lack in information. You can defeat your opponent with the hard evidence of their dirty laundry, but not with sloganeering. - Ralph Nader

The best Truthers – those who pose a real threat to any system of power - tend to be very pragmatic people. Above all else, they want to uncover the dirt that will bring their adversary down. Rather than dealing with injustice in the abstract, they prefer the hard proof of <u>this</u> particular wrong by <u>this</u> individual or group at <u>this</u> time and place. To find that evidence you must become a thorough investigative researcher, and know how to stubbornly persist over years in following leads, bits of information and hidden eyewitnesses, and putting the pieces together.

Research is not an easy task in a society like ours where information is increasingly monopolized, compartmentalized and controlled by governments and corporations, and is thereby effectively out of public reach. Nor will your conditioned habit of looking for truth from mainstream sources, or over the computer, be of any help to you. Cyber sources like the internet are tightly monitored and controlled, and allow you to see only what the system wants you to see. Truth lies much deeper. But where?

Evidence of corporate crime, or malfeasance by any group of people, is always hidden in three places: confidential records, physical evidence, and in the knowledge of eyewitnesses. The first source is normally outside your reach, but the other two are not. And so as a novice truther you can readily uncover proof in certain places and certain people.

Places are where you must begin, for eyewitnesses do not tend to step forward easily or quickly. A witness to a crime normally has either already being threatened or fears that he will be, and so waits for some guarantee of protection before he will disclose what he knows. But a crime scene is not guided by such human frailties. It exists. It can be found and its secrets revealed, with the right procedure and expertise. And after all, its hard physical evidence is what any court of law considers to be conclusive proof of a crime, like a murder weapon, or a cadaver.

In short, start by asking yourself *"Where is the body?"*.

In searching for the trail of the killers of Indian residential school children, I began at the physical location of those death camps. I was fortunate that some eyewitnesses had already begun speaking publicly of the crimes they'd seen there, and these human sources often pointed me and other researchers to the exact spot where children had been buried, or other proof hidden. But because the perpetrators of the crime were the government and churches of Canada and the RCMP, these sites were quickly sealed off or dug up by the police. And so I had to keep falling back on the eyewitnesses to corroborate the archival and physical proof I was gathering. My research focus had to remain flexible, moving towards any new opening.

One thing I quickly learned was to not only expect no help from conventional research sources, like academic scholars or institutionalized "experts", but the active hostility and opposition of such groups. For by my research I was exposing the deficiency of their own.

As my findings made the press, my biggest critics were the official, state-approved "experts" on Indian residential schools, who labored under the mainstream "consensus" that the schools were not genocidal or intentionally criminal bodies. The hard proof – like the enormous death rates that spanned decades – contradicted that consensus. But rather than modifying their party line, the academics by and large showered disrepute on what I had proved, helped arrange my expulsion from my own doctoral program, and actively censored and shut down any discourse based on my work in their classrooms and campuses. *

And so, once again, when it comes to researching and proving any corporate crime, you must learn to become your own expert resource and seek out the sources that are neglected or deliberately concealed by the "official experts". You should gather a small team of research associates around you in this purpose, like idealistic college students who have the time and knowledge to root around archives, interview witnesses and search for crime scenes. These helpers are indispensable simply because of the normally huge workload involved in any competent research.

... .

* *Again, some of the details of this academic censorship campaign towards the proof of Genocide in Canada are described in my book **Unrelenting: Between Sodom and Zion** and at* www.itccs.org *. Because of this censorship, I was denied a doctoral degree at the University of British Columbia, and subsequently barred from lecturing on that campus even after being invited there by scholars. See the evidence they fear at* www.murderbydecree.com

Once you and they have hit pay dirt and found physical proof of a crime, you must resist the temptation to dive right in and pull out the evidence on your own. All that will do is destroy its pristine *in situ* condition and make it inadmissible as bona-fide evidence in any court of law or public inquiry. Instead, you must employ forensic specialists, trained archaeologists and scientific experts to systematically analyze your evidence and produce their own independent report on what you've found.

That can be the tricky part, not only because of the big expense in using such experts, who don't usually operate on a gratuitous basis. The very fact that these specialists are normally employed by universities, governments or corporations means they can be gotten to and intimidated easily, and stopped by the usual unseen forces. Precisely such a thing occurred at our first excavation of a mass grave at the Anglican Mohawk Indian school in Ontario during 2011. (*See* www.itccs.org *and www.murderbydecree.com)*

For this reason, the most reliable course is to find independently-employed specialists who aren't afraid of a controversy or risk surrounding you; or simply acquire the skills and knowledge yourself to uncover and analyze the evidence in a way that will satisfy a court or inquiry, and get the proof on an official record – including by holding your own public, independent inquiry into the crime.

The more you persist in directly uncovering evidence, the more you will be approached by random witnesses who will come forward, usually with trepidation and in confidence, to spill their guts about what they know. Their statements are as important, and perhaps more so, than any amount of physical evidence you may have unearthed.

In truth, these witnesses are the living proof of what you allege. A human story is always more convincing than a document or a description. *"I was there and I saw what they did!"* is what the perpetrator of any crime most fears to hear.

Getting witnesses to speak and recording their story is a fine art requiring great patience and persistence – and the intuition to sift out opinion from fact. It's an axiom in our work that witnesses and survivors of a crime never tell the worst part of their story first, since it's too painful and debilitating for them. They will tend to talk around the heart of what they know. And so while you must gain the trust of people before you can interview them, always keep gleaning from their account the bits of proof that will fill out your other evidence.

You'll also discover quickly how people will be one way when a video camera is not on and another way when it is.

When witnesses know they're being recorded, their manner becomes very strained and self-conscious. They will tend to clam up, and not name names or things that they feel may backlash on them later. After all, to them you're just a relative stranger who wants them for their story. You will have to prove to the witnesses over time that you are risking and have risked as much or more than they have to get the truth out.

Ultimately, everything is about trust, and encouraging them to see the importance of giving what they know a public airing.

What helps this process is to make it a group one. Whenever you can, gather other witnesses and survivors together in small, closed circles to share their stories. The fact that another person has gone through the same suffering or knows of the same wrong is very empowering for anyone.

This is because we all tend to believe that we are alone in our truth and our ordeals. Simply bringing witnesses together will catalyze their willingness to speak and go on record.

Two conditions are essential within such sharing groups: *absolute security and confidentiality*. People must not only feel safe to speak but assured that what they disclose will not be immediately blasted all over the public airwaves.

At the same time, it must be made clear to them that only by such exposure will a wrong be stopped. At some point you must request of the group members their written or oral permission to use their statements beyond the group. *You can never use a testimony of any witness without first obtaining such permission.*

This imperative is not simply due to a matter of ethics. It is also a way to cover your own ass from allegations that you are using peoples' stories without their approval: a common smear and bad jacketing claim that is routinely thrown at truth tellers by their adversaries.

When interviewing witnesses, always remember to have them be specific about everything. Have them name names, incidents, dates and people who can corroborate their claim. Record their statements on video and take simultaneous notes to highlight for yourself key aspects of their testimonies.

After awhile, your archive of testimonies and other evidence may become huge. *Never, ever, store single copies of anything in one place.* Your records are invaluable and must be copied and stored in separate, secure locations, preferably not at your home address or a location known to your adversaries.

Finally, when it comes to accessing confidential records held by your adversary or similarly unreachable location, your main hope is to find an insider who can open these sources to you. We find that such people inside the system do eventually come forward with such documentation, but only after years of your efforts that prove to them that you are genuine and reliable. Several such sources came to me from within the Canadian government and even the Vatican with damning proof of planned criminality by these institutions.

Another means of prying open secret archives and records is by publicly naming and shaming the institutions holding those files, compelling them to release some aspect of them – usually a much watered-down version edited by their lawyers. Such was the case when the Canadian churches "released" some of their residential school records after we had occupied their buildings and accused them in the media of hiding their crimes. What they issued was whitewashed and hid the real evidence of their child-killing practices; and yet the fact of having forced such a disclosure heightened the prestige of our campaign and compelled others, including some church insiders, to come forward.

I've found that the groups you would normally expect to be of help in your investigations do not prove to be so in practice.Take the much-touted "Public Interest Research Groups" (PIRG's), for example: one of the "official" public advocacy forces reputedly devoted to exposing corporate crimes. They have been known to do so, but always from a safe distance after searching through routine channels. PIRG's and their ilk tend to operate on campuses and engage in "acceptable" and safe forms of activism on mainstream environmental issues, for example.

Like Amnesty International, PIRG's also receive state funding and have ties with the very groups engaged in corporate criminality, especially governments and churches.

Ultimately, there is no substitute for the fact that, despite any help you can muster, you are the one who has to keep digging out the evidence and creating a public space for the issue. Your supporters will come and go, but only you know the issues behind your cause the best. And in your pursuit of the truth, persistence is your greatest weapon. In the long run, time will vindicate your efforts, as it erodes secrecy and lies.

Appendix Two: The Art and Rules of War
(With acknowledgement to Sun Tzu and Karl von Clausewitz)

A. Core Principles

1. The sole purpose of war is the annihilation of the enemy. To aim at anything short of this invites defeat.

2. Enemies, like all opposites, are mutually dependent on one another, being part of a greater unity and purpose. Thus, enemies are defeated not by their abolition but by their absorption into that greater whole.

3. Striking at the heart of the enemy is the ultimate doctrine for victory and has no substitute. All strategy must be directed towards this purpose.

4. Purpose precedes action and must never be shaped by it. Defeat is assured when action precedes purpose. Battles are lost when purpose dissolves into random response.

5. Wars are won only when a unified leadership transforms random events into controlled outcomes, by purposely shaping such events.

6. One skilled in battle summons one's enemy and is not summoned by them; one skilled forms the ground of battle, and the enemy must follow; offers, and the enemy must take. Thus is the victorious army first victorious and then does battle, while the defeated army first does battle and then seeks victory.

7. Nothing is permanent in life except conflict and change. Therefore, nothing is permanent in war except uncertainty, the recognition of which must guide all strategy.

8. It is the nature of war that swiftness rules. Everything will be won with swift action at the key moment, or lost without it.

9. Power is found not in solid or predictable things but in the constant flow of relationships, which are always changing. The power of a squirrel to cross a river on a log lies neither in the squirrel nor the log, but in their momentary combination. That temporary combination is their power.

10. Every additional link required in the attaining of an objective causes delay, confusion and failure to increase exponentially. Every link removed from the achieving of an objective causes clarity, vigor and success to increase exponentially.

11. Knowing the enemy and knowing yourself: in every battle, no danger. Not knowing the enemy and knowing yourself: one defeat for every victory. Not knowing the enemy and not knowing yourself: in every battle, certain defeat.

12. There can be no reliable defense in war, since any defensive posture invites attack.

B. Strategy

13. Engagement with an enemy cannot be avoided. Warfare by its nature compels direct engagement. Maneuver is an unreliable means to final victory, and being a tactical consideration, is but one aspect of a command strategy.

14. Nothing will demoralize and defeat an army primed for battle quicker than avoiding a direct engagement with an enemy. Therefore, all maneuver must always be aimed at and result in such rapid engagement.

15. An army that sees fear or indecision in its commanders will collapse. Chain of command is sustained fundamentally by the valor and determined example of the commanders, and by their demonstrated capacity to grapple directly with the enemy and triumph.

16. Shock attack is preferable to stealth, since such a shock maximizes an army's impact as well as the fighting spirit of its troops, while restricting the enemy's options and capacity to attack.

17. To receive a blow, even when prepared, is to be weakened by it. One can only gain victory through the offensive. Defend and one is insufficient. Attack and one has a surplus.

18. Seasoned enemies expect and are trained for the unpredictable, and cannot be easily ambushed, decoyed or misled. Win victory therefore through naked force aimed at an enemy's weakest point.

19. The morale of one's troops is a key but a shifting and random factor in battle, and can only be established by the strong leadership of the commanders.

20. Whoever depends on a majority for victory must reflect its weakest aspects and must thereby be defeated.

21. Seasoned minorities alone are capable of sustained and purposeful action and thereby, victory. Only veterans are capable of victorious combat, by leading the inexperienced or wavering mass in their wake. The leadership of this vanguard of veterans is the key to victory in every battle.

22. Victory is formed by the strategic command but is won by the operational commanders. The quality of these secondary leaders and their cadres is fundamental to any victory.

23. When I am few and my enemy is many, I can use the few to strike the many because those whom I battle are restricted, being larger and more unwieldy. Their strength thereby becomes their weakness.

24. The clarity and will of the commander forms the ground of the entire army; and such clarity comes from personal honesty and realism. The commander must never issue ambiguous or contradictory orders but act only from his own clarity, calmness and will.

25. Always carefully discern the enemy's purpose. The knowledge of the enemy comes only from active contact with them. Provoke them to reveal themselves, assessing their nature and responses. Prick them and know their movements. Probe them and learn their strengths and deficiencies.

26. Never reinforce error or defeat. Let your understanding move fluidly with each new experience. There is never a final or definitive outcome to the army that moves like water.

27. By being without permanent form and fluid in your movements and tactics, you compel your enemy to defend against you at every point. He is thereby dissipated and weakened, and kept ignorant of your purpose while forced to reveal his condition to you.

28. By this means of formlessness, you can force the strongest enemy to conform to the ground you have chosen for it, on the terms of your victory. But without foreknowledge of the ground itself, none of this is possible.

29. Therefore, active reconnaissance and good intelligence before any engagement are essential to victory. The commander who acts without knowing the enemy and the terrain first invites disaster.

30. Engage an enemy with what they expect, so that what you allow them to see confirms their own prejudices. This settles them into predictable patterns of response, distracting them from your actions while you wait calmly for the extraordinary moment: that which the enemy cannot anticipate or prepare for, being confirmed in their patterns.

31. Be in this manner invisible and unfathomable to your enemy. To be thus without form, first be so orthodox that nothing remains to give you away. Then be so extraordinary that no-one can predict your action or purpose. Use the extraordinary to win victory.

32. Ride the inadequacies of your enemy. Go by unpredicted ways. Attack where your enemy has not taken precautions and avoid where they have.

33. Bind your own army to you with deeds. Do not command them with words.

Tactics-Operations

34. Successful tactics are the offspring of true experience but must always remain supple and expendable. Tactics are by their nature transitory; if they become enshrined into a permanent strategy or doctrine, they are a recipe for disaster.

35. Operations must always be geared to the rapid seizure and exploitation of the key moment of opportunity created in battle, which can never be predicted. The prime purpose of operational commanders is to recognize and act decisively upon such fleeting moments.

36. An unshakeable will to pursue victory using every opportunity is the one essential quality of tactical commanders, and tends to overcome every setback or unforeseen event.

37. Before engaging an enemy, form the ground of battle on terms favorable to you, then shape the ground to deceive the enemy, with actions that fit the enemy's own mind and situation. Thus you form victory before and during battle by always standing on your own ground.

38. Never repeat successful tactics or maneuvers with the same enemy, or they will recover and adapt to your tactics.

39. Do not respond to the ground your enemy has prepared for you, but instead, shape their ground. Then they have no alternative but to be led by you, as if it was their own idea.

40. Hide the time of battle from an enemy, and make what he loves and defends your first objective. When near, manifest far; when able, manifest inability, so as to confuse him.

41. Let your plans be as dark as night, then strike like a thunderbolt with utter surprise. Prior to such a surprise attack, feign weakness and offer the enemy a truce, to lull his defenses. The unexpected attack always negates the superior strength of an enemy.

42. Respond to aggression by creating space, so as to control the actions of the aggressor. Resist, and you swell the attacker. Create room for the aggressor and he will dissipate.

43. When aggression by a superior foe remains undissipated despite your actions, engage the aggression by guiding it into conditions favorable to you. Feign retreat to draw his forces into traps.

44. Use order to await chaos, stillness to await clamor. At the right moment, not acting is the most skillful action.

45. Hostile ground heightens your focus. Cut off from home support, you take nourishment from the enemy and learn self-reliance. Such supply lines cannot be severed. Use the threat surrounding you to stay united and inspire your army.

46. Place your soldiers where they cannot leave, and have no alternative but to fight or die. Facing death, they find their true strength and cannot be routed. When they cannot leave, they stand firm and fight. For thus do extreme situations cause your troops to find a deeper resolve and a source of inner power.

47. This deeper resolve cannot be taught or accomplished by training or commands. Dire circumstances automatically evoke it, unsought yet attained. Commanders must fashion these moments by using hopeless situations to their advantage. The right relationships, especially when facing disaster, unleash enormous power greater than the individual parts.

48. If a mightier enemy pauses though enjoying an advantage, they are tired. If divisions appear in their ranks, they are frightened. If their commander repeatedly speaks soothing reassurances to his army, he has lost his power. Many punishments indicate panic. Many bribes and rewards mean the enemy is seeking retreat.

49. Do not initially confront the enemy in their strength, but at the points of their weakness. These points are in constant flux and must be recognized and attacked with lightning speed.

50. In all engagements, aim at and seize something the enemy holds dear; then their strength and plans are rendered useless, and they must stop and respond on your terms. Likewise, whatever you love makes you vulnerable and prone to manipulation: prepare yourself to relinquish it.

Addendum: The Nature of Rear Guard Actions

1. Rear guard actions are required when an army is in retreat or maneuver and seeks to decoy an enemy by camouflaging its movements or weaknesses with a deceptive appearance of strength or initiative.

2. A rear guard action is inherently defensive and arises from desperation or weakness. An army advancing from strength has no need of rear guard measures. Only an army on the strategic defensive must screen its real aims and movements.

3. When an enemy detaches a portion of its army as a rear guard force, one must respond quickly and aggressively against the enemy since he is off balance and vulnerable. Yet one must never respond on the terms of an enemy's read guard force, which is merely a delaying decoy, but rather must push past such a force in order to strike at the main body of the enemy that is in retreat or maneuver.

4. Rear guard actions are temporary stop gap measures and are often improvised under desperate conditions, and thus cannot be relied upon to restrain for long an enemy's main body. Rear guard actions are accordingly a means of last resort, and since they will be recognized as such by a sage adversary, employing such a measure can invoke an undesired retaliatory response by an enemy that may render the rear guard ineffective and self-defeating.

5. For these reasons, rear guard actions must be employed very selectively and judiciously. By themselves they can never secure victory. They must be launched only in conjunction with a broader offensive strategy that seeks to overcome one's enemy not through deception and maneuver but by a redeployment that shifts the *shih* and strategic initiative to one's own army.

Appendix Three: Useful References

<u>The Art of War</u> by Sun Tzu (520 BC)

<u>On War</u> by Karl von Clausewitz (1832)

<u>Rules for Radicals</u> by Saul Alinsky (1971)

<u>Unrelenting: Between Sodom and Zion</u> (2016) & <u>Murder by Decree: The Crime of Genocide in Canada</u> (2016) by Kevin D. Annett [www.murderbydecree.com]

<u>Meditations</u> by Marcus Aurelius (178 AD)

<u>Man's Search for Meaning</u> by Victor Frankl (1953)

<u>Action for a Change</u> by Ralph Nader (1971)

<u>Agents of Repression: The FBI's Secret Wars Against the Black Panther Party and the American Indian Movement</u> by Ward Churchill (2002)

The FBI COINTELPRO Operations published by The Public Eyewitness http://www.publiceye.org/liberty/Feds/cointelpro.html

<u>Radio Free Kanata</u> – *www.bbsradio/radiofreekanata* – **every Sunday @ 3pm pacific, 6 pm eastern**

A Note on Existing Whistle blower Organizations

Canada and other "Crown" countries lack any independent advocacy system or defense organizations for whistle blowers or political dissidents. The existing Canadian "watch dog" or Ombudsman offices are all funded and controlled through the Provincial Attorney General's office: by the party in power.

However, if you live in America, there are a battery of groups, often government funded, that purport to aid and assist in-house whistle blowers. These groups rely on First Amendment legal defenses and established organizations like the American Civil Liberties Union and the Center for Constitutional Rights in New York City.

The focus of these groups is entirely on seeking resolutions for whistle blowers within the existing legal system and resolving differences with their opponents before arbitration or law courts. This approach has obvious pitfalls and limitations when your corporate adversary is out to destroy you through illegal and covert means, or if your opponent is the government itself.

An extra word of caution: These kind of "official" advocacy and support groups normally perform a monitoring role for the government and corporations by tracking dissidents like you. Bear that in mind when dealing with these groups and keep your cards close to your chest. The truth is that there is no sure-fire formula or guarantees for surviving as a truth teller. You are your own best solution.

About the Author

Rev. Kevin D. Annett, M.A., M.Div., is a veteran truth teller and Nobel Peace Prize Nominee from Canada. He is an award-winning film maker, author, radio host, community organizer and public speaker. Since 1995, when he was fired without cause from his pulpit by the United Church of Canada after exposing crimes by that body, he has successfully led the campaign to unmask and prosecute the genocide of aboriginal children by Canadian church and state.

Despite being blacklisted, impoverished and subjected to a massive smear and misinformation campaign by the RCMP and covert agencies, Kevin forced an official public "apology" for crimes in Indian residential schools from the Canadian government in June, 2008. In 2010 he helped establish the International Tribunal of Crimes of Church and State (ITCCS) which now operates in nine countries. Between 2012 and 2014, Kevin assisted in two common law court prosecutions of the Vatican, the Crown of England and others guilty of Crimes against Humanity, which compelled the forced resignation of Pope Benedict from his office in February, 2013.

Since January, 2015, Kevin has participated in the movement to establish a sovereign common law Republic in Canada and has hosted the public affairs program Radio Free Kanata. He operates community training schools for whistle blowers and other activists, and is a consultant with many groups of survivors of crimes by churches, governments and corporations.

Kevin is the author of eight books and co-produced the award-winning documentary film *Unrepentant* in 2007. He holds Masters Degrees in Political Science and Theology. Scholars in America and Europe have nominated him for the Nobel Peace Prize on two occasions.

One man and the truth makes a majority.
Thomas Paine, 1778

Copies of this Manual can be obtained from the author
and at www.createspace.com or Amazon.com

Messages can be left for the author at 386-323-5774
(USA).

www.murderbydecree.com , www.itccs.org

hiddenfromhistory1@gmail.com

Made in the USA
Middletown, DE
03 September 2020